T0187351

CYBER CRIME AND WARFARE
ALL THAT MATTERS

CYBER CRIME AND WARFARE

Peter Warren and
Michael Streeter

ALL THAT MATTERS

ALL THAT MATTERS

First published in Great Britain in 2013 by Hodder & Stoughton. An Hachette UK company.

First published in US in 2013 by The McGraw-Hill Companies, Inc.

This edition published 2013

Copyright © Peter Warren, Michael Streeter 2013

The right of Peter Warren and Michael Streeter to be identified as the Authors of the Work has been asserted by them in accordance with the Copyright, Designs and Patents Act 1988.

Database right Hodder & Stoughton (makers)

All rights reserved. No part of this publication may be reproduced, stored in a retrieval system or transmitted in any form or by any means, electronic, mechanical, photocopying, recording or otherwise, without the prior written permission of the publisher, or as expressly permitted by law, or under terms agreed with the appropriate reprographic rights organization. Enquiries concerning reproduction outside the scope of the above should be sent to the Rights Department, Hodder & Stoughton

You must not circulate this book in any other binding or cover and you must impose this same condition on any acquirer.

British Library Cataloguing in Publication Data: a catalogue record for this title is available from the British Library.

Library of Congress Catalog Card Number: on file.

10 9 8 7 6 5 4 3 2 1

The publisher has used its best endeavours to ensure that any website addresses referred to in this book are correct and active at the time of going to press. However, the publisher and the author have no responsibility for the websites and can make no guarantee that a site will remain live or that the content will remain relevant, decent or appropriate.

The publisher has made every effort to mark as such all words which it believes to be trademarks. The publisher should also like to make it clear that the presence of a word in the book, whether marked or unmarked, in no way affects its legal status as a trademark.

Every reasonable effort has been made by the publisher to trace the copyright holders of material in this book. Any errors or omissions should be notified in writing to the publisher, who will endeavour to rectify the situation for any reprints and future editions.

Typeset by Cenveo® Publisher Services.

Hodder & Stoughton policy is to use papers that are natural, renewable and recyclable products and made from wood grown in sustainable forests. The logging and manufacturing processes are expected to conform to the environmental regulations of the country of origin.

Hodder & Stoughton Ltd

www.hodder.co.uk

Contents

1

The nature of cyber crime

Cyber crime (or cybercrime as it is also often written) is an inelegant term used to cover a whole range of different offences and activities carried out by individuals, gangs, businesses and, in some cases, governments, with the aid of new technology. For many, the phrase is simply an alternative to 'computer crime' – that is, any crime involving the use of computers, either as a tool of the crime or the intended target. But that usage is becoming increasingly outdated as cyber crime also covers any illegal activities involving the Internet. Mobile phones and other handheld devices make use of the Internet without any involvement from computers – though, of course, one could argue that modern mobile phones or smartphones are simply mini-computers, even if we don't call them that.

So cyber crime refers to any offence committed using a computing device, personal computers, computer networks, the Internet in general, telecommunications systems, message boards, internal communications systems such as intranets and mobile devices, including smartphones. An important element of cyber crime is that – generally, though not always – the criminal acts are carried out remotely, with a distance between the criminal and the victim. So, for example, someone disseminating a computer virus – a classic cyber crime – could do so from the palm-fringed beach of a tiny remote island, many hundreds of miles away from their nearest potential victim. This, evidently, can make the criminal harder to catch. Cyber crime is, in that sense, a natural development in crime for a world that has become more globalized. Whereas once government, the military and the financial community were the only ones who were able to make decisions remotely that affected people a long way away, now criminals have that power, too.

▶ New crimes or old?

Are cyber crimes simply more high-tech versions of old 'real world' ones, or new offences? This is a good question and the answer is – in most cases – the former. Identity theft is cyber crime. It lies squarely at the heart of it. You use someone else's details to gain access to places that you should not be – assuming another person's identity to gain access to their money and other valuables. This is not new, as criminals have been using such techniques since the dawn of time. However, the modern practice of putting so much personal and financial information on computers, data storage devices and online has made identity theft a much easier and thus more lucrative crime. It is much safer for the criminal, too, as often they can assume the identity of someone on the other side of the world, reducing their chances of getting caught to almost zero.

Another example is stalking, another familiar crime that has now found online form in what is called 'cyber stalking'. It's the same as 'real world' stalking except that it's easier to carry out, as the stalker doesn't have to leave the comfort of their living room.

On the other hand, one could argue that hacking – the use of computers and the Internet to gain access to someone else's electronically stored data – does not have any real-world parallels. Yet, as we shall see in the next chapter, computer hacking originally evolved from the 'hacking' of telephones, known as 'phone phreaking', which was not itself at the time illegal. Perhaps a better example of a 'new' form of crime would be computer viruses. If you used a time machine and travelled back even just to the 1960s, you would have a hard job explaining to someone what a computer virus was. Nonetheless, that person would understand the notion of sabotage – which is effectively what viruses help commit.

In general, then, we can say that cyber crimes are largely traditional forms of crimes using modern tools. After all, at some point in the past highwaymen graduated from using knives to guns, so it should come as little surprise if, in the 21st century, some of them are now upgrading to computers. The essence of the crimes remains the same: bad people wanting your money, individuals wanting to victimize others – as in stalking – or societies and companies wanting to steal their competitors' secrets.

The major cyber offences

Identity theft	Computer fraud
Hacking	Cyber espionage
Computer viruses	Software piracy
Denial-of-Service (DoS) attacks	Cyber stalking and bullying
Phishing	Child pornography

As in the so-called real world, some cyber 'crimes' are in the eyes of the beholder. So, for example, protest movements in repressed countries have turned to the Internet and, in particular, social media to communicate with each other and the outside world. The 'Arab Spring' of 2011 was a good example, with protesters against the regimes in countries such as Egypt and Tunisia making extensive use of social media; the uprising in Tunisia even became known as the 'Facebook Revolution'. For the states in question, however, these communications were considered subversive and thus cyber crimes. On the other side of the coin, there are some civil liberties groups who consider that *any* state surveillance of the Internet, emails, websites and so on is a cyber crime (in the moral if not the legal sense), whether carried out by dictatorships or Western democracies.

Western governments and businesses have also been targeted by politically motivated activists or 'hactivists' who seek to embarrass the authorities or companies through targeting and taking down official websites or releasing confidential information. Anonymous is perhaps the best-known of these hactivist groups. For the authorities, such activities are a 'crime'; for the activists, they are a simple manifestation of their liberty of expression and protest, and there have been (fruitless) attempts to enshrine it as such in the US Constitution.

Another example of what some consider moral cyber crime is unauthorized file-sharing, the practice of downloading music, films and other data from the Internet and sharing it with friends or 'peers' without permission from the copyright holders. For some this is natural sharing of material, akin to giving a friend your newspaper or magazine to read. But for the music or film industries this is a breach of their copyright. In the United States the 1998 Digital Media Copyright Act (DMCA) made the exchanging of files of copyrighted material illegal. Four years later the US Department of Justice said it would prosecute cases of so-called 'peer-to-peer piracy'. Thus, for the American authorities, such activity is indeed a cyber crime.

One important factor to consider in relation to cyber crime is the fundamental nature of the Internet and the World Wide Web. The Internet – the telecommunications infrastructure – and the Web – the system that displays pages via HTML, or Hyper Text Markup Language – enables any user to go where they want online and even remain anonymous. This is in line with the philosophy of the early adopters of the Internet (and later the Web): that it should remain free, open to all, egalitarian and non-commercial. It may be hard to imagine now, but early on commercial use of the Internet was frowned on by many users. This philosophical approach to the Internet has many laudable aspects to it. It has encouraged, for example, the use of the Internet as a tool against oppression, as discussed earlier. There is also the idea that the pursuit of knowledge should be a private endeavour. There are also civil liberties groups who consider that any collection of our personal information online by firms for commercial purposes – so-called data mining – is itself a cyber crime.

But the anonymous and chaotic nature of the Internet – who runs it? who controls it? who polices it? – is also of great benefit to criminals. The ability to commit crimes at distance without one's identity being known – or at least requiring considerable effort to get it – is a technological windfall for them. In Dickensian London, pickpockets were able to commit crimes, then vanish into the rat-run of tiny streets to escape pursuers. Using the Internet, criminals do not even have to leave those rat-runs. For some law enforcement agents, the World Wide Web is synonymous with the 'Wild Wild West'.

The anonymous nature of the Internet and the Web has also encouraged individuals to behave in ways they would be reluctant to do – for fear of being caught – in the real world. So, for example, free, anonymous and virtually unlimited access to pornography on the Web has led to a truly colossal number of hits on porn sites. It has been said that the porn industry worldwide is worth more than the combined revenues of Microsoft, Google, Amazon, eBay, Yahoo! and Apple.

This furtive interest in pornography makes Internet users more vulnerable to criminals, either through blackmail – criminals find porn searches when they hack a computer, then threaten the owner that they will reveal it – or, more often, through users visiting websites that then download malicious software that surreptitiously sifts through private and financial information on that person's computer.

▶ A big problem – but how big?

The true scale of the problem of cyber crime is hard to quantify. In July 2012 General Keith Alexander, the director of the National Security Agency, which oversees United States Cyber Command, America's military organization fighting cyber attacks, suggested that the total cost of loss of intellectual property to American companies alone was around $250 billion a year. Internationally, the figure was said to be $1 trillion dollars, though the figure is highly controversial. However, these figures – mostly based on computer security company reports – have been widely contested as being far too high. The British government has itself estimated the annual cost of cyber crime to the United Kingdom's economy at £27 billion, but again some experts have disputed this figure and say it is an exaggeration.

The truth is that it is virtually impossible to put a true and accurate figure on the cost of cyber crime to society. For one thing, individuals and especially companies do not always know whether they have been targeted and lost out, financially or commercially. Even when home-owners and firms do know they have been hit, they may not report the loss, perhaps through embarrassment or for reasons of commercial confidentiality. However, even just using conservative reported figures, the numbers are huge. The United States' Internet Crime Complaint Center (IC3) has put the annual cost of Internet crime based on complaints made to it at just over $485 million. Another way of assessing the financial scale of the problem is that the value of the computer security industry worldwide is put at around $300 billion annually.

Despite the uncertainty over figures, what we can say unequivocally, however, is that cyber crime now poses

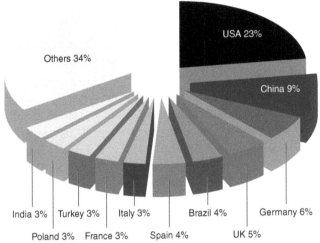

India 3% | Turkey 3% | Italy 3% | Brazil 4% | Germany 6%
Poland 3% | France 3% | Spain 4% | UK 5%

▲ Pie chart showing the countries suffering the most cyber crime
(Source: http://www.enigmasoftware.com, 18 April 2013)

the greatest potential threat to our society that we have even known. Why? It is because of the massive global uptake of technology at the end of the 20th century by businesses desperate to save costs and boost productivity. In embracing the world of, first, computers and then the Internet the world adopted technology that lacked the empirical certainty of the cogs of metal and drive shafts of the Industrial Revolution. It was a completely new idea. In the Industrial Age we had grown used to a spade being a spade – now we were in an age where a good spade could be a bad spade at the press of a button. Computer code is a language and it can be adapted and rewritten by others, and for dubious purposes.

▶ The Internet's original sin

The fact that we were working with an imperfect technology was not at first realized; the possibility that we might be doing bad things with computer code was simply not considered. Thus, from the very beginning, the world of computing and the Internet was based on imperfections, flaws and sometimes poorly understood processes. You might even call this the Internet's 'original sin'. Eventually, not just 'intellectual' hackers and computer philosophers were exploiting these faults, but criminals, too.

By then it was too late. By the early 21st century the modern world has become utterly – one might say frighteningly – dependent on computer code and the Internet. From cars to public utilities, from nuclear power plants to the buildings we live and work in, all rely on the digital world to function. Unfortunately, by allowing the imperfection into the system from the start, the creators of this world also let in the criminals, terrorists and rogue states. These groups have learned how to exploit the technological weaknesses that underpin our daily lives, in ways of which we are largely ignorant. Cyber crime is today a threat to our very way of life.

This last point has not been lost on military strategists. Taking out a country's water supply system could be even more effective – and cheaper – than dropping plane-loads of bombs or firing endless quantities of hugely expensive rockets. The Prussian general Carl von Clausewitz famously said: 'War is the continuation of politics by other means.' As we shall see in a later chapter, cyber attack is now the continuation of war by other means.

2

The history of hacking

When teams of highly talented mathematicians and academics worked together at Bletchley Park in central England during the Second World War to break German military codes, they were carrying out work of the utmost importance. By cracking the codes used by the German Enigma and Lorenz machines, the code-breakers are estimated to have shortened the war by up to two years. Nowadays the Bletchley Park site is home to the National Museum of Computing, but it is also a popular venue for 'geek' and hacking events, paying homage to the men and women who once worked there. Why? Because many hackers see those wartime teams as 'predecessor code-breakers', their spiritual forebears.

In the recent past, hacking – the unauthorized entry into a telecommunications system, network, computer or database – was an intellectual game and was not a crime. The motivation for it was the same as climbing a mountain for mountaineers – because it was there. Modern hackers come in all shapes and sizes; some still do it just for the thrill, many do it for money, while still others are political idealists. But whatever their motivation, hackers are the most visible, best-known and, it has to be said, the most glamorous of all cyber 'criminals'.

The modern hacking movement originated in the 1960s in the United States. And it did not involve computers – which were still very much in their infancy then – but the telephone system. Talented, technologically minded and intellectually curious youngsters – some of them students at the prestigious Massachusetts Institute of Technology (MIT) – learned how to hack into the telephone system. This meant they could talk to people all around the world for free. Most of these early 'phone phreakers', as they were called, were idealists who were not hacking phone networks to save or make money. Instead, they were engaged in a voyage of discovery to understand exactly how the system worked, acquiring knowledge and insight that rivalled and sometimes surpassed that of telephone engineers. In fact, they would occasionally pass on information to the telephone companies about system weaknesses they had found, and actively disapproved of other students who used 'phreaking' simply to avoid paying phone bills.

But the line between 'good' hackers and the less ethical could become blurred. An example was John Draper, who left the US Air Force in 1968 and who went on to become a legendary phone phreaker. His main motivation was intellectual curiosity. In a magazine article in 1971, Draper explained that for him a phone company was simply a 'system' to explore. He said that if he does what he does, it is only to explore a system. 'That's my bag,' he said.

The US authorities saw things rather differently and Draper was twice prosecuted, the second time in 1976 when he served a short prison sentence in California. Here the intellectually curious hacker came into contact with hardened criminals. They became interested in Draper's ability to hack phone systems, not, it is safe to say, out of scientific curiosity but because they saw that they could make money out of it. So Draper's cell became a kind of 'hack school'. Criminals also asked other phreakers to build them hacking devices. Hacking – or at least some people involved in it – had moved to the dark side.

▶ Famous hackers

As mentioned, the so-called 'good' hackers were primarily interested in spotting and exploiting flaws in systems to make an intellectual point, and to highlight how the system could be improved. They loved technology and wanted to make it better. This relationship between hacking and the development of the computer (and later the Internet) is a close and important one. Steve Wozniak, the co-founder of Apple Computers, was himself a phone phreaker (in the days before it became illegal), apparently inspired by reading the magazine article on John Draper referred to earlier. At a speech in 2004, Wozniak explained the appeal of hacking for many: He described hacking as often just about a kid trying to be funny, and explained that hackers have a particular sense of humour. 'Most people just don't get our jokes,' he said.

Another figure with a hacking past is Tim Berners-Lee, the man who designed the Internet protocol that became the World Wide Web at the start of the 1990s. While studying at Oxford University, he and a friend were caught hacking and banned from using the university's computer system. It is also worth noting as an aside that, after developing the World Wide Web, Berners-Lee declined to take out a patent on his creation, preferring it to be free and available to all. In this, we can once again see a key hallmark of the Web (and the Internet) – their free and ubiquitous nature, which springs from the philosophy of those who helped develop them. One other prominent person with an ethical hacking background is software engineer Linus Torvalds, a Finnish American who was the driving force behind the open-source – non-proprietorial – computer operating system LINUX. Even Bill Gates – the co-founder of mighty Microsoft – was one of four school students temporarily banned from using computers at the now defunct Computer Center Corporation (CCC) after the company found that they had exploited bugs in the operating system – essentially a form of hacking, legal at the time – to gain additional free time on its computers.

The transition from phone phreaking to computer hacking came about as a direct result of improvements in telecommunications technology. As phone systems became reliant on ever more sophisticated computers to work them, so the phone hackers had to learn the language that these systems used – the code behind the UNIX operating system. Eventually, then, the attention of hackers switched from the phone system itself to computers – and the data stored on them.

What hackers do

A hacker is a person who breaks or 'hacks' into a computer or communications network or database. They use the Internet and computer software to probe the weaknesses in their victims' defence system and break inside. Once inside, they may use other software to send back key data or destroy or disable systems, depending on their motivation. But hackers don't just use technology; they often rely on human skills to glean passwords or other useful information enabling them to hack into a system. Traditional hackers say their primary aim is to take something apart to find out how it works and to see if they can improve it or adapt it to their purposes.

Gradually, too, the hackers began to attract the attention of the media as well as the authorities, and during the 1980s some high-profile cases caught the public imagination and for the first time raised the spectre of hacking as a serious issue for society.

One eye-catching series of hacks was carried out in 1983 by a group of youngsters aged 16 to 22 when they found their way into 60 different computer systems across the United States. The most high-profile of their targets was the centre for nuclear weapons research at Los Alamos. Though the gang did not gain access to any sensitive information during the Los Alamos intrusion, the hack alarmed the government. The FBI tracked down and arrested the group, and they were all subsequently put on probation. When asked about why they had carried out the hacks, one of the group said: 'It was more curiosity than anything else.'

The hacks themselves had not been that sophisticated. The youngsters had simply dialled into the computer systems using the old Telenet phone network and then used the system's passwords. They were able to do this because the default manufacturers' passwords for these systems had not been changed – and in most case were very basic and easy to guess. This is a crucial point that helps explain why the modern world is so vulnerable to cyber crime; the basic framework for computer networks and many computer chips and devices were not built with security in mind. They were designed as, and expected to remain as, closed systems to which only authorized people had access. This was fine as long as these systems remained self-contained and not connected to the rest of the world. But, once they could be reached first by phone networks such as Telenet and then by the Internet, their vulnerabilities were exposed to the whole world.

▶ Social engineering

However, the vulnerability of the modern world to cyber crime is not simply a result of defective technology or technological genius on the part of the hacker. Human frailty also plays a role. Many hackers who have infiltrated computer systems do so using a mixture of technological skills and tools and human skills. Typically, they make contact with personnel at the organization that is being targeted and glean information that might be useful in working out passwords or codes, perhaps by posing as an employee of a client company, as a friend or relative of a member of staff or as a supplier. This kind of subterfuge has been given the rather grand name of 'social engineering'.

A hacker who made particular use of social engineering was Kevin Mitnick, a man who was once on the FBI's most-wanted list and who carried out a series of high-profile hacks in the 1980s and 1990s across the United States. Fascinated by technology and very able at the technical side of hacking, Mitnick was also gifted at coaxing information out of unsuspecting employees. Over the course of nearly two decades, Mitnick was said to be responsible for hacks on firms such as Motorola, Nokia and Sun Microsystems, as well as organizations such as the University of California. His exploits were alleged to have caused tens of millions of dollars of damage. Mitnick was perhaps rather better at hacking than he was at evading the clutches of the law. He was twice jailed for hacking, the second time in 1999, having been on the run from the FBI for two and a half years, and then being kept in custody for another four. Later, Mitnick explained his views on hacking. 'It's a skill set,' he said. He explained that people from different walks of life can use that skill, saying they can use it for a criminal purpose, or to 'exercise their curiosity or their interest' and to learn more about a particular area.

▶ Hacking goes criminal

However, by the time Mitnick was operating, the authorities in the United States, the United Kingdom and elsewhere in the world had come to the conclusion that hacking was a criminal act per se, and all perpetrators faced the risk of prosecution. The idealistic time of the 'purist' hacker was over.

Yet, although the prosecution authorities decided to pursue hackers, it took some while for the criminal law to catch up with them. In 1984 two Britons hacked into an electronic mail system called Prestel (which has long since vanished). Their crime may have been overlooked had it not been for the fact that the two men, Robert Schifreen and Stephen Gold, succeeded in hacking into a mailbox belonging to the Duke of Edinburgh, husband of the British monarch Queen

Elizabeth II. The duo were charged and convicted under the 1981 Forgery and Counterfeiting Act, but later acquitted on appeal. In 1988 the appellate courts ruled that neither man had forged, stolen or damaged anything, and thus they were, under existing law, not guilty of any criminal offence.

The result was new legislation, the 1990 Computer Misuse Act, which among other things made it a criminal offence to gain unauthorized access to computer material. Similar legislation, meanwhile, had been passed in the United States six years earlier in the form of the Computer Fraud and Abuse Act. Hacking had become well and truly criminalized.

Ironically, although by the start of the 1990s hacking had been made a crime in much of the Western world, the criminal fraternity in general – the people who commit crimes to make money – had not for the most part become involved in hacking or other forms of hi-tech crime. There were a number of reasons for this. One was that, until the emergence of the Internet in the 1980s, and more particularly the World Wide Web in the early 1990s, relatively few organizations and hardly any private individuals were digitally connected to the outside world. Thus, opportunities to make money were restricted. Secondly, with crime gangs and syndicates doing well out of drugs, weapons and people trafficking, there was perhaps little incentive to move into an area with which few 'ordinary' criminals are familiar. A third and related reason is that to get involved in hacking and hi-tech crime you need to have certain skills – or least to know where to find others who have them.

So it was not until the mid-1990s that criminals began to move into the hi-tech domain in a more systematic way. One of the first recorded attempts of a hack on a bank was carried out by a Russian, Vladimir Levin, who was arrested in 1995 for hacking into Citibank accounts in the United States and transferring money into other accounts he and others had set up. Levin entered a plea arrangement with the US authorities and admitted to only one count of conspiracy to defraud and stealing US$3.7 million. One of the interesting features of this case is that Levin, who was based in St Petersburg, was supposedly recruited by a criminal gang to carry out the hack. It was later claimed that Levin himself was simply a middle man, having paid a local hacking group for details of how to get into the Citibank system. In any case, criminal gangs were beginning to learn; lacking the skills themselves, they had realized that their best way into the world of hacking was through recruiting experts, either through financial incentives or threats, or in some cases a mixture of both.

White hat/black hat

A distinction is often made in hacking terminology between 'black hat' hackers and 'white hat' hackers. White hat refers to so-called ethical hackers, often hired as consultants by companies to test the defence mechanism of their information technology systems. As long as they work with the permission of the company concerned, what they do is legal. Black hat refers to any hacker who breaks the law by gaining unauthorized access to a database, website, network or other information system for their personal benefit. Occasionally, the term 'grey hat' is used to denote hackers who penetrate a system to highlight a weakness, then offer to share their information with the organization or company that owns the system, for an appropriate fee.

While money-motivated hackers have taken up many of the headlines and occupied the efforts of law enforcement agencies, the ethical and politically motivated hackers have not gone away. Indeed, in recent years they have enjoyed something of a revival. Political hacking has had a particularly strong tradition in Europe. In what was then West Germany, for example, a group called the Computer Chaos Club (CCC) staged a series of high-profile hacks in a bid to embarrass the authorities and large state organizations whom the group regarded as 'oppressors'. For the most part, people affiliated to the CCC were, indeed, politically motivated, although some members later admitted selling West German industrial secrets to the Russian KGB for money, which rather undermined their credibility.

In the Netherlands, meanwhile, a magazine called *Hack-Tic* was at the centre of a group of politically motivated 'anarchist' hackers. Their philosophy was very much in tune with that of the early hackers or phone phreakers in the United States – that systems were there to be explored and that freedom of access and information were paramount. The magazine's founder, Rop Gonggrijp, explained his philosophy in a 1995 interview, when he said:

What matters to me are the ideas behind hacking – free access to information for everybody. In our society information is no longer stocked in libraries and archives but is burrowed in databases and spread over the network. It is a knowledge machine that ninety per cent of the population can't access.

A decade later, in 2005, he appeared to believe that the fight to have access to information stored on computers had gone badly when he gave a speech at a conference in Berlin entitled 'We have lost the war', although in 2010 he partially backtracked on that pessimistic claim.

Gonggrijp has since been involved with the whistle-blower site WikiLeaks. Although WikiLeaks is not itself a hacking organization, it sits squarely within the old hacking philosophy that information should be free and freely accessed, hence its decision to publish thousands of classified documents from countries around the world. Its founder, Julian Assange, was himself also a hacker. And WikiLeaks actions have been publicly supported by some of the most prominent hacking activist or 'hactivist' groups of recent years, including Anonymous and its offshoot, LulzSec. Anonymous is a loose organization – even that may be putting it too strongly – of like-minded hactivists who have become involved in a number of high-profile campaigns and online attacks.

3

The rise of the Internet and the virus threat

ALL THAT MATTERS

If hacking had become familiar to the general public by the mid to late 1980s, it took a little longer for computer viruses to make their mark on society. But when they did, from the early 1990s, it marked the dawn of a new era for computer users. No longer could they use their email and visit websites unthinkingly. Instead, they had to be aware that they were under the near-constant threat of attack. It was the age of mass cyber crime or, if you prefer, mass cyber vandalism.

The term 'vandalism' seems quite appropriate for viruses and their impact because they have an indiscriminate effect on potentially hundreds of thousands or even millions of computer users, regardless of who they are and where they live. Just as we all have to suffer from the actions of 'real world' vandals who break windows, deface street walls or rip up train seats, so we all have to live with the consequences of computer viruses. This is one of the reasons why many hackers – who are perfectly happy to justify breaking into computer networks and databases – show contempt for those who write and release virus programs. The least skilled of these writers are often referred to as 'script kiddies'. The expression is not meant as a compliment.

Yet the very notion of a computer virus, which is a program able to replicate itself and move from one computer to another, has an academic history of impeccable credentials. It was the brilliant Hungarian mathematician John Van Neumann (1903–57) who first came up with the concept of viruses as long ago as 1949. He did not use the term 'computer virus' – that was to come much later – but his essay on the 'Theory of

Self-reproducing Automata' was essentially a blueprint for a self-reproducing computer program. That was before the computer age had really begun, so the idea remained just a theory for two decades.

The first virus is generally thought to be the Creeper virus written by Bob Thomas, who was working at a US firm in 1971. This was an experimental program designed deliberately not to damage but to test mobile applications, and was not called a virus. Nor did it exist outside the company. The first virus believed to have made it into the 'wild' was called Elk Cloner, which was written in 1981 and which affected only Apple II computers using the Apple DOS 3.3 operating system.

▶ The rise of the Internet

The annoying Elk Cloner was not at the time described as a 'computer virus' as the term was not yet in use. That came two years later in 1983, when Fred Cohen, a research student at the University of California, created one in the laboratory and then used the words 'computer viruses' in a paper describing his experiment. The expression was not Cohen's invention – it had been used in classes by one of his teachers at UC, Leonard Adleman – but now it had been made public and caught on. The computer virus had become official.

Viruses now had a name, but it was to be some years before they had a real impact on much of the world. True, the first virus for IBM PCs was written in 1986, apparently by brothers who owned a firm called Brain

Computer Services in Lahore, Pakistan. The brothers intended only to stop infringements of their software, but they created a virus. However, the virus's biggest 'limitation' – and that of other viruses at that time – was that it could reproduce itself only slowly. This was because Brain (as it was called) infected a computer via the floppy discs that in the early days of mass computing were used to 'boot up' PCs and load data. Thus, the virus could be spread only slowly. For viruses to have maximum impact, they needed to have easy access from computer to computer. They needed the Internet.

The history of the Internet goes back rather further than many people think. As early as 1962, the American computer scientist J.C.R. Licklider had put forward the idea of linking different computers to form a network. Within a decade a variety of what were called 'packet-switched' networks had been developed, of which the most important was called ARPANet, standing for the Advanced Research Projects Agency Network.

The 'ARPA' part was an agency of the United States Department of Defense, and this was not the first or last time in history that military projects have led to developments of great benefit to society. The idea of ARPANet was to connect computers at laboratories in universities and research institutes around the United States. Conspiracy theorists suggest that the real intention behind this creation was to create a network that could withstand a nuclear strike. In fact, the real reason was rather more prosaic. At the time, ARPA had only a limited number of powerful research computers at its disposal and these were scattered around the country, making access hard for researchers. Joining them together would simply speed up research.

ARPANet began life in 1969, initially just connecting computers within the United States, but in the early 1970s first Norway and then the United Kingdom were connected. In 1983 the US military split off from the project to form their own separate communications link. Meanwhile, various computer scientists, including Vinton Cerf and Bob Kahn, worked on the protocols to harmonize the different networks that had begun to develop – of which ARPANet was one. It is hard to give a precise date for the birth of the Internet because it was an evolving process, but by the early 1990s it had come into widespread use. With the arrival of the World Wide Web in 1991 (widespread consumer adoption of the Web started in 1995–6), a significant part of the world's population was now exposed to the biggest network in history. At the same time, the scale and popular use of the Internet and Web – particularly in the form of exploding demand for emails – represented a giant opportunity for computer virus writers.

The potential vulnerability of both the Internet and users to attack – as we have seen, the security of the network was an afterthought – had in fact already been demonstrated in the late 1980s, when the Internet was still in its infancy. In this instance, the attack came not in the form of a computer virus but a computer 'worm'. Often the word 'virus' is used as a catch-all term to describe all methods of delivering an attack on computers and networks, including worms. But the worm is in fact a different kind of beast. Unlike the virus, which needed something to latch on to – a program or a document, for example – a worm was originally completely self-contained, a program in itself. Often, now, the two are used together in combined or 'blended' attacks.

Inherent weaknesses

The creation of the Internet was an evolving process. As a result, the entire network and its UNIX code was still in Beta, or test, form when it was rolled out and used by universities and the public. This was the reason for the proliferation of what are known as 'buffer overflow' weaknesses on websites that are exploited by hackers and viruses to inject malicious codes. These codes will infect a computer the moment the user tells it to open the website concerned. However, the original code used by the developers that was the root of this problem was very effective in doing what it was supposed to do and, due to the non-proprietory nature of the code, the weakness was not corrected until Version 7 of the Beta Code in 1979. It is also important to note that Microsoft software – the most popular commercial operating system – was not originally designed with the Internet and its potential security issues in mind.

The worm that nearly brought the early Internet to its knees was created by a Harvard graduate studying for a doctorate at Cornell University in 1988. Robert Tappan Morris came from an impeccable background: his father was a senior scientist at the US National Computer Security Center in Maryland. In 1988 the student found an apparent hole in the UNIX code used by computers and telecommunication networks. In November of that year, Morris decided to release a code of his own into the computer network, to test that weakness. He assumed that his code would go undetected. Unfortunately for him, his code had other ideas and the 'worm' that Morris created began to behave in an entirely unexpected way, replicating itself endlessly on computers as it spread across the ARPANet and into other local networks. It is estimated that around six thousand computers connected to the fledgling Internet were affected, with many systems administrators at some of the country's top research institutes being obliged to switch off their overloaded machines. It was a massive and salutary warning to the developers of the new world of the Internet – the realization that viruses and worms had jumped from floppy discs to the biggest network in the world, the Internet.

The World Wide Web

The World Wide Web was invented by the British scientist Tim Berners-Lee at the start of the 1990s and is essentially a system that allows us to see linked 'hypertext' documents or 'pages' from our computer. The Web is not the same as the Internet. The Web can be regarded as an application or service that runs on the Internet, which itself is a worldwide system of connected computer networks. Berners-Lee's key contribution was to devise how to make the already-known hypertext system work with the Internet.

▲ Tim Berners-Lee – inventor of the Internet

▶ The virus era

Robert Morris had not meant to bring the Internet to a standstill with what became known simply as the Internet Worm. His code was released out of intellectual curiosity, in the proud tradition of the early hackers. But he was unable to escape punishment and was fined $10,000 and put on probation for offences under the Computer Fraud and Abuse Act.

The Internet Worm was a foretaste of what was to come from computer code writers who either did not care what damage they caused or who actively sought to wreak havoc. Some were more effective than others in this. The Michelangelo virus of 1991, for example, was claimed to be a deeply damaging virus that could affect – and, according to some, had affected – hundreds of thousands, if not millions, of computer users. In fact, the virus, which remains dormant until 6 March each year (the birthday of the great Italian Renaissance artist Michelangelo, born 6 March 1475), when it overwrites part of the host computer's hard drive, affected only around 10–20,000 computers. Nonetheless, for a few years, warnings were issued to users that they should not operate their computers on 6 March.

More widespread were the so-called macro viruses that began to emerge in the 1990s. Previously, viruses had targeted a computer's operating system directly; the virus attached itself to a program and when the program ran so did the virus. Macro viruses, however, run *inside* a program. The virus writers caught on to the fact that many computer users use Microsoft Word documents and open them when they are sent as attachments by email. So the virus was hidden *within* the Word documents or whatever other program had been selected. When the document was opened, the virus ran.

The first macro virus of this type that attacked Microsoft Word was the Concept virus of the mid-1990s. But one of the largest of the genre was called Melissa. This virus appeared in March 1999 and exploited the massively increasing number of email accounts using the Internet. When email users received the Melissa email and opened the attached Word document, the virus was activated and went to the user's Microsoft Outlook email client – one of the most commonly used at the time – and sent the original email to the first 50 addresses in the address book. In this way, the virus spread quickly, probably more quickly than any virus up to that point, and infected perhaps as many as a million computers, clogging up and closing down their overloaded email clients.

The Kournikova virus

The Kournikova virus, named after the tennis player Anna Kournikova, was a well-known virus that was released in February 2001. Like many such viruses, it relied on 'social engineering'. Recipients of the bogus email saw a subject line reading 'Hi: Check this!' and an attachment called 'AnnaKournikova', with the virus writer hoping that many people would be tempted to open the attachment to look at a picture of the glamorous Russian. Many did. The young Dutch virus writer Jan de Wit quickly gave himself up to the authorities and was given 150 hours of community service. De Wit said he released the virus without thinking and without foreseeing the consequences, and he denied any intent to cause damage. An important aspect of the case is that, while De Wit 'wrote' the virus, he did so using a 'toolkit' that he had downloaded from the Internet. This is typical of the so-called 'script kiddies' who send out viruses.

An important feature of the Melissa virus was that, as well as using technology, it also involved social engineering. The wording of the emails made some recipients think that it had come from someone they knew, making them far more likely to open the attachment and trigger the attack. This form of social engineering was also employed in one of the most devastating of all viruses and worms. In 2000 the ILOVEYOU virus, also known as the Love Bug or VBS/LoveLetter, was launched on the world. Its impact was immediate and massive. Within two weeks, as many as 50 million computers were affected by this worm, as recipients were seduced by the subject message 'I LOVE YOU' and the attached love letter. Among organizations whose emails were affected were the British Parliament, the Pentagon and the CIA. This was an example of the malicious software, or 'malware', that really put viruses on the map.

Estimating the true damage caused by any virus or worm is notoriously difficult to do, so one must treat any such figures with caution. The harm done includes not just the direct damage to computers and the cost of repairing them but also the impact of the loss of working time on a company or an economy. The worldwide damage caused by ILOVEYOU, for example, was put at more than $5 billion.

No one was prosecuted for the ILOVEYOU worm, though a suspect was identified in the Philippines, a computer student from Manila called Onel de Guzman. However, de Guzman never admitted being behind the attack, and in any case at that time the Philippines had no law that made the sending of ILOVEYOU a criminal offence (a gap that was quickly remedied). This highlights an important point in the international fight against cyber crime. As the Internet reaches every corner of the globe, criminals can work from jurisdictions with either weak laws or poor law enforcement, meaning that the rest of the world can do little to apprehend them.

Since the emergence of the mass worms and viruses of the 1990s, such attacks have continued on a huge scale, even though media interest in them has waned. Only a handful of the tens of thousands written and released have caused significant damage, either thanks to antivirus (AV) software protection or the fact that the viruses were poorly written in the first place. One notable worm worth mentioning was MyDoom in 2004, a fast-spreading worm carrying out multi-pronged attacks. No one is quite sure who wrote MyDoom or what its central aim was, but it was designed to leave 'back doors' open in computer security systems, allowing the attackers to return and leaving the system vulnerable to other viruses.

Thus MyDoom fits well with the changing face of cyber crime that occurred in the 2000s. Certainly, neither the idealistic hacking nor the mindless vandalism of indiscriminate viruses had vanished from the scene. But, increasingly, they were being overshadowed by attacks motivated either by money or by politics, both personal and international. It was in this decade that individual criminals and organized crime began to move into cyber crime. For them, cyber viruses are not an end in themselves but a means to an end – money.

▶ The commercialization of cyber crime

Organized crime and individual criminals gradually began to realize that not only were there vast amounts of money to be made in computer and Internet-related crime, but there was another important bonus in such crimes. This was the low risk of being caught, particularly if you were based in parts of the world where the law was not always fully enforced.

Organized crime gangs began actively recruiting the technological workers they needed to commit cyber crime, for example in cities such as St Petersburg where, after the collapse of the Soviet Union, there was a growing number of unemployed but very talented computer experts. In a sense, these gangs began to operate in ways similar to the process occurring in the technology crucible that is Silicon Valley in the United States, with one crucial difference – their emphasis was on criminal technological innovation.

Criminals provided the technologists with the seed capital to build their systems and stipulated that they wanted to see a return on investment and/or they guided the experts towards particular activities that would be useful to them – such as money laundering and running pornography websites. Overall, organized crime's message was that it wanted to see the development of innovative criminal activity – in other words, making lots of money with new technology.

This led to the development of a criminal industry that mirrored the activities of the legitimate technology industry and even extended the range of services that were available. So, while legitimate Internet businesses offer telehousing – the hosting of servers in a protected and managed building now known as a data centre – organizations such as the Russian Business Network, an organization 'founded' in St Petersburg but whose present location is unknown, offers 'bullet-proof' or ultra-secure hosting to the purveyors of hardcore porn and illegal sex sites.

Other groups worked on the development of criminal databases specializing in the bulk sale of stolen identities, the provision of a network to deliver spam email, and extortion – all based around the evolution of the computer virus. Usually, each group specializes in one field and sells those services in much the same way that the legitimate computer industry has partitioned itself, selling antivirus and firewall products, web hosting and software applications, and often selling them as a suite of bundled products.

So, for example, one group would work on developing viruses to infect computers and take them over, creating what is known as a zombie computer – a computer used for online criminal purposes without its owner knowing. This searches the computer for any useful identity information and houses it on a collection server. It is then part of what is called a 'botnet' to be used in cyber attacks (see Chapter 6).

For the victims – us – the threat is ever present and growing. A bewildering array of different types of 'malware' is constantly being developed by the criminals and their technology-smart co-workers. In just one month in 2012, 280 million malicious programs were detected around the globe. Nor do computers come under threat only *after* they have been bought and connected to the Internet. In December 2012 there were reports that brand-new computers made in China had been 'pre-fitted' with sophisticated malware by criminals before they had even left the factory gates. Cyber crime is now a big and sophisticated business.

4

Industrial cyber espionage

Cyber espionage is one of the most important, emotive and controversial areas of cyber crime. It is also a broad-ranging area. The term can be used to cover the stealing of industrial and commercial secrets, by rival firms, criminal gangs or, in many cases, states. In this chapter the term 'cyber espionage' is essentially used to refer to a high-tech version of industrial espionage. However, cyber espionage can also refer to attacks carried out by states on other states or strategically important sites such as nuclear power stations or military bases. This is discussed in Chapter 10. Naturally, there is some overlap between the two. For example, states may indulge in industrial cyber espionage not simply for narrow commercial purposes but for wider geopolitical reasons, too, namely to boost their national economy and thus power, while weakening their rivals.

▶ Cyber crime big and small

Cyber espionage is the corporate arm of high-tech crime. It primarily involves attacks not on individuals but on companies and institutions. However, cyber espionage is not always necessarily carried out on a large scale. It may simply involve a firm hiring someone to snoop on a competitor by sitting outside its offices in a car to see if they can hack into that company's wireless network and thus read communications and access data. Wireless networks are often poorly protected, or not protected at all, by secure encryption. Or a criminal may hire someone to gain access to a firm's headquarters, plug a USB storage device into a computer terminal and infect that firm's network with malicious software that seeks out and sends back valuable information on the company to the gang. The losses resulting from such data theft can be crippling for individual firms. In many cases, the vulnerability of such companies to cyber espionage of this type is due to poor understanding of security, a lack of appreciation of the value of the data that a company holds, and changing workplace habits. There will be more on this later.

▶ 'The biggest wealth transfer in history'

The small-scale attacks carried out on firms, outlined above, are indeed a major problem. But the industrial cyber espionage that is really worrying policy-makers, law enforcement agencies and large corporations is the high-tech spying that is taking place on a global scale, and which is targeting the industrial secrets of many of the world's top companies. Such attacks involve the use of computers to probe their intended victims' networks, either directly seeking information or, more likely, seeking to infect those networks with malware that will seek out and transmit the information back to the attackers' computers. Often, such attacks come from countries many thousands of miles away.

As we mentioned earlier, in July 2012 the United States Army General Keith B. Alexander, the director of the United States' National Security Agency, called this form of cyber crime 'the greatest transfer of wealth in history'. By this he means that unscrupulous foreign (non-US and generally non-Western) criminal gangs and states are hacking into the databases of top companies in the United States and other Western countries. They are doing so in search of patents and copyrighted designs – intellectual property – and price-sensitive information and other data.

In his speech, Alexander went on to quote some figures on the cost of the loss of intellectual property (IP), including a $250 billion annual bill to US companies alone and a figure of $1 trillion globally to fight cyber crime. As already noted, these figures are disputed by some experts. Nonetheless, that there is a massive problem of intellectual property and data being stolen wholesale from the West is not really disputed. 'That's our future disappearing in front of us,' as General Alexander put it. A year earlier the general had revealed that a US firm lost $1 billion of intellectual property in the course of just a few days during a sustained cyber attack.

In the United Kingdom there is similar alarm at the scale of the problem. In June 2012 Jonathan Evans, director general of the UK's security agency MI5, warned: 'What is at stake is not just our government secrets but also the safety and security of our infrastructure, the intellectual property that underpins our future prosperity and the commercially sensitive information that is the lifeblood of our companies and corporations.' The British spy chief revealed in his speech that in just one single case a 'major London-listed company' had lost £800 million because of a cyber attack launched by a foreign state. The authors understand that the company lost the money because a £800 million contract fell through after the attackers stole intellectual property. The head of Britain's spy communications centre GCHQ, Iain Lobban, also revealed in 2012 that a leading global pharmaceutical company had seen a five-year, £1-billion research programme severely compromised after product data was stolen in a cyber attack. This allowed a cheaper rival product to hit the market first.

▶ The Chinese connection

Who is behind this colossal attack on (mostly) Western intellectual property and commercial secrets? In some cases, it is undoubtedly the work of criminal gangs. However, some of the larger and most sustained of the so-called 'advanced persistent threats' (APTs) are clearly carried out by structures that have greater resources than the gangs – states.

The identity of these states willing to hack into other nations' computers, though, is a highly sensitive subject. If one questions Western government officials on the record about who is behind these APTs, they are usually extremely reluctant to point the figure at individual nations, and for good reasons. One reason is that it is indeed notoriously difficult to uncover precisely where such attacks are coming from. Sophisticated attacks can be pinged around many different points or 'nodes' on the Internet before hitting their target, making it hard to pinpoint the true origin. Another is that it is difficult to know at what level of seniority within a state these attacks are sanctioned, or even if senior ministers have any knowledge of them at all. Despite this, however, experts called in to investigate such attacks generally have a very strong suspicion – if not always actual proof – of the likely geographical origin of the APT.

Advanced persistent threats

An advanced persistent threat (APT) is the jargon used to describe a sustained and serious attempt by a major cyber attacker – a state or a large criminal gang – to target a particular network or series of networks belonging to the victim. APTs typically involve the use of sophisticated malware as part of their armoury but often include social engineering as well. The term is thought to have been first coined by US Air Force analysts in 2006.

The other reason why officials are so reluctant to discuss publicly where the attacks come from is political. Two countries often mentioned as being a significant source of cyber attacks are Russia and North Korea. But, while Russia is an important player on the world economic and political scene, its importance pales in comparison to the country that most experts believe is the origin of many of the biggest cyber espionage attacks – China. China's importance as a world economic superpower and its sensitivity over being blamed for such attacks are the main reason why most Western governments are so cautious about pointing the finger of suspicion.

But not all countries or politicians and certainly not all organizations are so coy. In 2009 Walter Opfermann, an espionage protection agent for the state of Baden-Württemberg in Germany, named China as the country behind many of the industrial espionage attacks that were costing Germany around €50 billion and 30,000 jobs a year, although he also named Russia as another offender. The German official said that the industry sectors most targeted included car manufacturing, chemistry, optics, renewable energies, communication, x-ray technology, materials research and armaments.

Opfermann said cyber espionage was the technique increasingly being used by China and Russia to glean industrial secrets, citing the use of Trojan programs – software often contained in spam or bogus emails that infect computers and search for and transmit valuable data back to the attackers. However, he said that old-fashioned 'real world' techniques were also used, such as phone-tapping, stealing laptops during business trips, or sending spies to infiltrate companies.

So why should countries such as China and Russia want to take part in industrial espionage on such a grand scale? The reason is time and money. By stealing Western technology and know-how – some of the information stolen includes management and marketing techniques – countries can trim years and billions of dollars off their own research and development process, an area that emerging countries are traditionally weak in. Opfermann pointed out that, for China to achieve its aim of becoming an economic superpower by 2020, it needs to acquire urgently the high-level technological information already available in developed industrial countries.

China – and Russia – strenuously deny being behind such attacks, but that does not stop the accusations being made. In a detailed 2012 report catchily entitled 'Crouching Tiger, Hidden Dragon, Stolen Data', from the independent security consultancy Context Information Security, blame was laid squarely on the Chinese. Referring to the many attacks against governments and businesses since at least 2003, the report states: 'By far the largest sponsor of these attacks is the Chinese state.' While accepting that the origin of cyber attacks can be hard to pinpoint, the report says it is happy to assert Chinese responsibility for many of them. 'If something looks, walks and quacks like a duck, it is almost always a duck,' the authors wryly note.

▶ China – the source of the attacks?

A key point that the Context Information Security report makes is that such cyber attacks – which it refers to as 'targeted attacks' rather than ATPs – are not random:

> These attacks are designed to steal information that will fulfil a clear set of requirements set by the Chinese state and furnish them with political, commercial and security/intelligence information. These requirements are carefully and clearly identified, shared with a number of government departments and constantly updated.

The report also notes that the areas being targeted by the state-sponsored hackers are those that have already been publicly identified in China's Five-year Plan and National Outline for Medium- and Long-term Science & Technology Development. In effect, these have become shopping lists for the hackers. The targets include the 'electronics, telecoms, manufacturing, extraction, energy, biotech, pharmaceuticals, aerospace, space and defence' sectors.

In 2013 another report, this one from the security company Mandiant, claimed to have identified the building from which many such hacking attacks emanate. This, it says, is a 12-storey nondescript office building in Shanghai belonging to the People's Liberation Army (PLA). The report claims that a hacking network known as Comment Crew or the Shanghai Group is based inside the building's compound. The Xinhua News Agency – the Chinese government's official press agency – dismissed the Mandiant report as 'amateurish', saying its conclusions were 'baseless'.

In the United States, a high-profile report to Congress from the United States–China Economic and Security Review Commission has similarly named China as the world's leading cyber crime culprit, calling the nation the 'most threatening actor in cyberspace'. The 2012 report claimed:

> Hackers in China have waged aggressive cyber espionage campaigns targeting a wide range of U.S. and international military, government, commercial, and other non-governmental organizations... [T]hese hackers seek to compromise targets ranging from smartphones to deployed military platforms, such as naval ships at sea.

In response, Chinese officials accused the commission of 'prejudice' and a 'Cold War mentality'.

In 2012 Mandiant estimated that more than one-fifth of Fortune 500 companies – the United States' top-earning corporations – had experienced recent serious breaches or were dealing with them at that time. However, it is hard to get detailed information on just which firms get hacked and what exactly is stolen, because the companies who are victims are often reluctant to admit they have been targeted. For example, the chemical giant DuPont was hacked – apparently by Chinese hackers – in 2009 and 2010. However, they did not make this news public, and details emerged only after, ironically, confidential emails on the subject between the company and a private cyber security firm were leaked on the Internet by the hacking group Anonymous.

American businesses are not, of course, the only targets of such attacks. Over a sustained period starting in November 2009, the networks of at least five leading American and European energy companies were targeted by hackers based in China. The victims were said to include ExxonMobil, Shell, ConocoPhillips and BP. In these cases, the object of the attack seems to have been highly sensitive information about the quality of the firms' oil reserves and the ease with which they could be accessed. The cyber security firm McAfee dubbed the attacks 'Night Dragon' and said they targeted computers in Kazakhstan, Taiwan, Greece and the United States.

An interesting point made by McAfee is that the attackers – believed to be based in or near Beijing – used relatively 'old' techniques, not state-of-the-art methods. These included spear-phishing – using targeted emails purporting to be from trusted sources – exploiting known susceptibilities in Microsoft Windows operating software and social engineering.

Two years after those attacks, in 2011, the US APT specialists FireEye claimed it had detected Chinese hacking gangs involved in cyber attacks purchasing data from Russian cyber crime gangs – the first time ever that such a crossover has been detected.

Spear-phishing

Spear-phishing refers to attempts by cyber criminals to retrieve user names, passwords and other sensitive information through emails that appear to come from a trusted source, and is commonly used in cyber attacks on businesses and other organizations. The attackers will often do their homework first, using social networking sites to discover relevant personal details about an individual before targeting them with an email. The more authentic their email seems, the more likely they are to succeed in gaining the trust of the recipient and thus getting them to open the email and any attachment with it. Cyber crimes nearly always include a human element, with attackers employing 'social engineering' to glean information. This is because humans – and human behaviour – are often the weakest links of any security system.

A highly effective spear-phishing attack was developed for one of the most notorious and high-profile APTs seen – against the company RSA. The 2011 attack on RSA is especially significant because the firm is a computer and network security specialist that provides security encryption, and its technology is used by many of the world's largest companies, by US and UK government departments and many others. The hackers managed to obtain the cypher keys (known as 'seeds') that sit at the heart of the RSA technology that encrypts sensitive information. Being able to breach the code of the most trusted encryption supplier in the world was clearly a huge security breach.

Yet this daring attack was successful not because it used dazzlingly clever hacking technology but because it targeted any company's biggest security vulnerability – its staff. Over a period of two days two emails were sent to two small and closely targeted groups of employees. Most of the emails were binned. But the mails were sufficiently convincing to persuade one staff member to retrieve the mail – which had the words '2011 Recruitment Plan' in its subject line – from their junk folder and open the attached Excel file. Once opened, hidden software installed malware on the employee's computer, which began trawling the RSA network for access and information.

▶ The human element

As stated, the RSA attack underlines the importance of the human element in cyber attacks. Companies can ring their networks with the most sophisticated defences, but these count for nothing if the firm's staff unwittingly allow the attacker past those defences. One issue that needs highlighting in this context is the changing way that people work.

Nowadays many people use work and home computers and mobile devices interchangeably. Work is carried out at home on personal computers while leisure activities – such as visiting social network sites – are carried out at work. On the face of it, this may seem harmless enough. But storing personal data on work-based computers renders employees much more vulnerable to someone wanting to gain access to a company by social engineering or as a means to initiate an introduction. Employees also often ask to use their own personal machines or favourite technologies at work – a trend known as 'consumerization' or the BYOD ('bring your own device'

▲ Employees are often the weak spot in any company's cyber security.

to work) culture. They claim knowing their way around a system improves their productivity. But this, too, can make them and the company more vulnerable to attack – perhaps by unwittingly importing malware from home.

But none of this can or should excuse manufacturers from ensuring basic security in the first place for their devices, or companies from making sure that staff work in a cyber-secure environment, with both the correct training and equipment. As General Alexander noted in his 2012 speech: 'We have this tremendous opportunity with the devices that we use. We're going mobile, but they're not secure ... our companies use these, our kids use these, we use these devices, and they're not secure.'

5

Identity theft and the curse of spam

Nowadays, information is the real currency. The Internet provides a good example. It is true that to get access to the World Wide Web most of us have to pay a relatively modest monthly payment to an Internet Service Provider (ISP) or a mobile phone company. But after that, the vast majority of the Web, and the sending and receiving of emails, is free.

On the face of it, that seems a good thing, and we rarely, if ever, spare a thought for the massive structure of the Web and Internet and how they are financed and maintained. But of course there is a price to pay. As Vanessa Barnett, a technology and media lawyer at the London-based law firm Charles Russell, notes: 'There's no free lunch on the Internet and the modern currency is not pounds, shillings and pence but personal data.'

Which is why just about everyone out there on the Web who runs a commercial website is after our personal information. There is nothing intrinsically sinister about this, as for the most part the reason websites and organizations seek information about us is to enable them to be more efficient in selling goods, services or whatever it is they sell. It is true that some of the big online players such as Google and Facebook have in the past come under fire for the way they have handled people's personal data. However, it is a two-way process. We are not obliged to give information to websites – we choose to do so in return for something we want, a service we want or access to a particular page or document. What we fail to understand is that, in effect, we are taking part in a commercial transaction, just as if we were paying for something with money; in this case the 'money' is simply our information.

The problem is rather like lottery winners who go on a spending spree – too many of us are overly free and easy with the personal information we share. For reasons that are not entirely clear, many Internet users are happy to part with details that they would not dream of disclosing over the telephone or in a face-to-face conversation. Perhaps it is something about the intimacy of being online with just us and the computer screen or our mobile phone, but we readily trust online websites and brands with our data. Indeed, people have shown that they are more willing to entrust personal information to Facebook and Google than they are to provide the same data to governments. In 2011 the German government announced that it intended to increase the amount of information collected during its population census, a request that provoked an outcry. But the German people now provide more information to Facebook than was requested by the authorities. This trust applies to our machines, too. We load huge amounts of sensitive and unique data about ourselves on our computers, laptops, mobile phones and tablets without a moment's hesitation.

Why this matters is that it is not just the Googles and Facebooks who want our information – criminals do, too. While the public at large may have been slow to grasp that information is the 'new oil', criminals have quickly realized its value and have flocked to the places where this information can be found in abundance, the World Wide Web. Many of them are what are called 'identity thieves'.

▶ How identity theft works

Identity theft is at the heart of cyber crime, not only providing a means for making colossal amounts of money in its own right but also producing the information that can be used, for example, in industrial espionage (see Chapter 4) and other forms of crime. ID theft is certainly nothing new but, thanks to the staggering amounts of data stored on computers and other devices and the ease of communication via the Internet or mobile phone networks, the practice has now become industrialized. The figures involved are colossal. In 2011, for example, the United States Justice Department said that identity theft had affected 8.6 million households over the previous 12 months. The total direct cost to families was put at $13.3 billion. Naturally, not all of these cases involved cyber identity theft. A good number would have involved 'old-fashioned' techniques such as criminals rifling through households' rubbish bags for information such as old bank and credit card statements. But the figures involving online identity theft are nonetheless huge.

Cyber identity thieves work with the same raw material and in a similar way to legitimate online businesses. In the legitimate world, lists of people – consumers – are highly prized, especially if those lists have been verified for accuracy and provide contact details. It is the same on the dark side of the Web, the shadowy world of cyber criminals dubbed 'Silicon Hell' by some.

The first thing that cyber criminals do is to steal lists of people's details, notably email addresses. They do this by:

▶ hacking websites and companies for databases

▶ employing site or web-scraping software – this involves the writing of special programs designed to 'scrape' useful details from websites. For example, to collect email addresses programs will be created to seek the '@' symbol used in email addresses. This is sometimes also known as 'web harvesting' or 'web data extracting'.

Thus, criminals spend a great deal of their time and effort in acquiring and compiling databases of information on private individuals. But, just as in the legitimate world, not all databases are equally valuable to criminals. The most prized are those verified as having up-to-date information on real people with 'live' email addresses. Large companies and governments go to a lot of trouble to ensure that their databases are as up to date as possible but they are the hardest to steal – this was one of the reasons for the glee in the cyber criminal world that greeted the theft of Sony databases containing details of up to 100 million people in 2011.

On the other hand, databases that are unverified and old may be of limited value to criminals. These differences are reflected in the prices for which criminals buy and sell such databases to each other in the twilight zones of the Web. On these shady websites, where wannabe hackers and virus writers can acquire all kinds of 'tools', verified up-to-date databases fetch much higher prices than those of doubtful quality.

Once they have acquired or compiled the databases, criminals cross-check them against other information on the Web using more web harvesting, the aim being to 'purify' the list to make it as valuable and useful as possible. Social networking sites are commonly used for this cross-checking, as people tend to update their entries on them regularly. In other words, the criminals are exactly mirroring how the legitimate marketing operations of large companies operate.

Other ways of collecting or cross-checking data are through snaring people into free online games sites and offering illegal downloads. Similar methods are used when free applications (apps) and other 'free' bits of software are offered. In an investigation by Bit9 in 2012, it was found that over a quarter of the apps on Google Play (who do not insist that apps are checked before they are sold) can access personal data such as contacts and email – 100,000 Android apps were found to be 'suspicious' or 'questionable'. Once collected, one way of using the data is for spam emails (see below) to persuade the unwary recipients either to hand over financial details directly or, more likely, to visit a website that has been infected with forms of malicious software or 'malware' that will automatically search for such information on that person's computer. The use of emails purporting to come from known sources or organizations is known as 'phishing'. The Bit9 report's findings underline the need for users to take responsibility for data they are prepared to divulge online or to software producers.

Phishing is a technique used by cyber criminals to persuade people to divulge their personal data, including, perhaps, their bank account details. Typically, it is done by sending out emails purporting to be from a financial institution, which then invites the recipient to fill in their details on a website. These details are then harvested and used to steal from that person's bank account or credit card. Often the mails are poorly written and easy to spot as hoaxes, but the best ones can be quite sophisticated and use familiar logos, typefaces and language to fool the recipient. The term comes from the notion of 'fishing' for victims, with the 'ph' perhaps a reference to phone phreaking (see Chapter 2).

▶ Credit cards

The main way that cyber identity thieves make money is through gaining access to people's bank accounts, by phishing for example, and by gleaning enough information about a person so that they are able to use their credit cards to make purchases. Clearly, the most valuable information of all to steal is credit card records.

An example in 2012 involved a husband-and-wife team from New York, Amar Singh and Neha Punjani-Singh, who were among the ringleaders of what was said to one of the largest and most sophisticated identity theft cases so far seen in the United States. Amar Singh, who pleaded guilty to identity theft and corruption charges, and his wife were among 111 people arrested the previous year, in a scam that pulled in around $13 million.

They received detailed credit card information from Russia, China and the United States on individuals and then used a team of shoppers to go out and use counterfeited cards on shopping sprees. Interestingly, Singh and Punjani-Singh, who pleaded guilty to petty larceny, appear to have used a mixture of old and new identity theft techniques. Some of the credit card information came from so-called 'skimming' devices used by criminal associates at restaurants and shops. Others came from malware-infected websites that had snared unwary visitors. Amar Singh was given a five- to ten-year jail term while his wife was given a conditional discharge.

The returns on phishing and other forms of social engineering used to commit identity fraud can be high, even if the response rate to the bogus emails is very low. Typically, attackers might send out 200,000

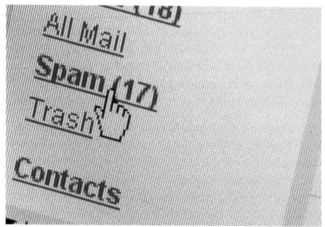

▲ While in itself not illegal, spam – unsolicited bulk email – is a key vehicle for Internet fraud.

emails to get just one 'hit' – someone who responds to the information by handing over bank details or by visiting a website where their computer is harvested for information. Often the sums stolen in an individual attack may be quite modest, perhaps just a few thousand pounds. However, even if there are only one or two successes a day, every day for a year, the total 'rewards' can be very attractive for criminals. And because the criminal is often in a different legal jurisdiction – often a different continent – from the victim, the work of law enforcement agencies is that much harder, making such crime relatively low-risk.

However, cyber criminals do not have it all their way all the time – the authorities and commercial organizations under attack can, and do, fight back. For example, when phishing attacks became widespread in the first half of the 2000s they were seen as a major problem for banks and credit card companies, who often shoulder the burden of any losses through identity theft. The problem was that phishing was a new phenomenon and a small but significant number of unaware customers were responding to the bogus emails. However, thanks in part to awareness campaigns and high-profile cases involving phishing – as well as improved software used by both banks and customers – in 2011 the UK's credit card companies were able to report a 22 per cent year-on-year fall in online bank fraud, to £46.7 million for 2010. This was despite the fact that the number of phishing attacks had increased by 21 per cent over the same period. Clearly, education of the public and improved security techniques had made a difference.

However, in figures reported for the first half of 2012, the same credit card authorities reported a 28 per cent increase in online banking fraud compared with the same period 12 months earlier. 'This has been driven by a huge increase in the number of phishing websites set up by criminals as part of a scam to trick customers into visiting these fake websites and disclosing their online banking login details,' said a spokeswoman.

This mixed outcome on online banking fraud in the UK highlights an important aspect of cyber crime, the way in which the authorities are constantly playing catch-up against the criminals. The authorities are often good at blocking a common criminal ploy online, only to find that the criminals have suddenly moved on to new, and perhaps more sophisticated, techniques. Meanwhile, each year there is a new batch of Internet users coming online, a percentage of whom will not be aware of the risks from online fraudsters until it is too late.

A revealing insight into the mind of an online identity thief came in 2011 in an interview that creditcards.com website carried with convicted ID thief and former fraudster Dan DeFelippi. He revealed that, when he carried out phishing attacks in the early 2000s, it was relatively easy to get a response because people were unaware of the fraud technique. DeFelippi (now a Web developer) also disclosed how easy it was to get hold of email addresses for his scams. He explained that there is software that harvests emails addresses from anyone who has ever entered their email address online. So he warns people never to put their emails on a website.

▶ The Zeus program

The sophistication of online criminals has increased markedly since the time when DeFelippi, who was convicted in 2004, was operating. For example, in recent years a sophisticated program called Zeus has been developed by cyber criminals. Zeus is a new development – a franchised crime system that is built according to the amount of money that the buyer has. The more money they have to invest, the more the system will be customized. Zeus – which is both a Trojan program and a botnet (see Chapter 6) – delivers stolen data back to those who are using it, assembles it into data packages for sale, and then turns the computers it has infected into a botnet. In essence, Zeus is an off-the-shelf 'crimeware' developed for those cyber criminals who do not have either the skill or the time to write their own programs.

What is particularly interesting about Zeus is that it breaks open banking systems and looks for data and that it can also be configured to intercept ID information for Government websites, including tax credits and student grants. The authorities in various countries have tried to attack the Zeus program and in 2010 a number of arrests were made around the world, including, in the US, of criminals using the crimeware. But the creator or creators of Zeus have yet to be caught. Indeed, they have even issued an upgrade to the system which allows mobile phone numbers to be gathered and matched with account data and other information. Once again, the parallels with the way in which the legitimate world of commerce works are striking.

The 419 frauds

Nigeria has gained an unenviable reputation as one of the world centres for fraud. Such crimes are known there as '419 frauds', named after the article of Nigeria's penal code that deals with those kinds of offence. The 419 fraudsters predate the Web and became infamous for writing unsolicited letters around the world asking for upfront funds to help release a large sum of money of which the recipient was promised a share. Needless to say, anyone foolish enough to send money never heard from the group again – unless it was to ask for yet more cash. With the advent of emails, such scams – known as advance fee frauds – have become extremely widespread.

▶ Spam

Spam is an unsolicited email sent in bulk that is usually advertising some product or service. In 2010 a joint United States–Chinese task force set up with the aim of fighting spam argued that a spam message had four clear attributes. These are:

1 Being uninvited by the recipient

2 Being high in volume

3 Being distributed widely

4 Being in the form of an electronic message.

It is a phenomenon that nearly all of us live with on a daily basis, a seemingly inevitable irritation on a par with houseflies and the common cold. For most of us, it appears little more than that – an irritation. But, in fact, the sending of such emails does not merely clog up the Internet with unwanted junk, waste energy and time, and cost the Internet infrastructure billions of dollars in extra costs – it is also the cornerstone of online crime, forming one of its main revenue streams. Spam is also one of the main methods for infecting computers and harnessing them for other criminal activities, as we shall see in Chapter 6.

These unsolicited messages can work in several different ways: they may

▶ infect the computer they are sent to with malware

▶ direct the recipient to a website that will infect their computer

▶ send the recipient to a website where they will buy some legitimate service

▶ take the recipient to a website where they can buy some illegitimate service.

One common factor is that spam is targeted at the unwary, the ignorant and the unprotected – essentially, the vulnerable.

Despite massive efforts by the authorities, spam is not likely to disappear any time soon from our in-boxes. In the early 2000s spam accounted for around 90 per cent of all email traffic. This figure has declined to around 70 per cent or even less – but, even as the old sources of spam are taken down, new ones spring up. New countries emerge as the kings of spam, too. Traditionally, that dubious title has been held by the United States.

However, in 2012 a report by cyber security firm Sophos said that India had overtaken the United States, spewing out some 10 per cent of the planet's least favourite emails.

Another development in spam has been SMS or text spam on mobile phones. At first glance, this may seem odd. The main reason why email spam is so popular for spammers is because emails are free to send; therefore there are virtually no overhead costs for the spammer. SMS messages, however, do cost money. It is thought, though, that the relatively low cost of sending texts in countries such as the United States, combined with the fact that people respond in number and quickly to SMS spam messages – people trust their mobile phones – has persuaded spammers that SMS spamming is economically viable. In 2012 there were reports that some SMS spam gangs were making up to $6,000 a day in the United States.

The rise of the botnets – the greatest threat to the online world?

The aspect of cyber crime that is perhaps the strangest – as well as the scariest – is the phenomenon known as 'botnets'. The current authors have likened them to wild 'herds' ('bot herds') rampaging around the Internet looking for systems to attack under the direction of anonymous 'bot herders' or 'bot masters'. It is the point at which cyber crime meets the world of science fiction. Yet even with botnets the crimes they are used to commit are straightforward enough, extortion and identity theft being the main offences.

So what exactly are botnets and are they really the greatest potential threat to the online world? First thing, the odd name. The name 'botnet' comes from the blending of three words, 'software robots' (or 'bots') and 'network'. These words give us an important clue about what botnets are and what they do. Botnets are networks of automated programs that have taken over or 'infected' computers, which are then controlled and used for specific ends via the Internet. An individual computer that has been taken over or 'compromised' by a bot is often described as a 'zombie' computer. The computer may become infected through the person using it opening an attachment on a spam mail message or visiting a dangerous website. In either case, a form of malicious software, or 'malware', downloads on to the target machine and sets up its own self-contained system. Think of those sci-fi films where alien creatures take over human bodies; the effect of a bot on a computer is not dissimilar. Once installed, the 'incubus' program is ready to become part of the wider network – the botnet – controlled by the bot master.

An important point is that the compromised computers could belong to anyone (or at least anyone whose computer is not well protected against cyber attacks). It could be our parents', our friends', even our own computer. Their location or who owns them is less important to the botnet owners than the fact that it is a computer connected to the Internet and which has its own IP (Internet Protocol) address. Many people continue to use their computer without realizing that it has become part of a botnet, though often this kind of 'infection' will harm a computer's performance. This explains why computer security experts and governments are so anxious to encourage computer users to ensure that they have up-to-date computer security systems in place.

The computers that make up a botnet do not need to be near each other. They can be, and often are, scattered all over the world. These malicious networks can be big, too. Typically, botnets may contain thousands of infected computers, but some may have hundreds of thousands or even more than a million. The bigger they are, in theory the more damage they can do.

So how do botnets work and what are they 'for'? Well, as with most things to do with computers, the Internet and the Web, bots started out as something benign. They were automated programs designed to help manage Internet Relay Chat (IRC): chat sessions for instant messaging. However, soon attacks on IRC began, leading to the development of malicious bot programs that turned individual computers into 'zombie' computers. From there it was but a short step for people – criminals – to start co-ordinating these infected computers into networks. By the start of the 21st century the botnet had been born. IRC sessions are still often used by botnet controllers to communicate with their 'herd'; they switch locations quickly, and often from chat session to session, to avoid being detected.

Early bots and botnets

The first bot was created in 1993 and was called EggDrop. It was a benign bot designed to help the running of Internet Relay Chat (IRC). The first malicious or bad bot, called Pretty Park Worm, was discovered in 1999. Like viruses and worms, botnets are given names by the computer security industry, although there is no agreed formula or process governing which names they should have.

Though the 'herding' and controlling of botnets is a sophisticated operation – and getting more so every year – as a cyber 'weapon' botnets can be something of a blunt instrument. Often they work by simply overloading a network or a website. The bot herders co-ordinate the computers within the botnet to send out requests for information to the designated target, for example a website. Just one or two, or even a hundred, repeated requests for information from a computer will not harm the website. But when it becomes hundreds of automated requests coming from networks of hundreds of thousands of computers, this can overload the targeted site. The result is system death; buried under an avalanche of requests, the website servers – the computers where the website is hosted – grind to a halt and collapse. Such attacks – and there are variations on this approach – are known as DDoS, or 'distributed denial-of-service', attacks.

The power of a botnet lies in its collective strength. The reasons why criminals want to use botnets to take websites offline or slow them down are varied. One is simply extortion. In traditional 'real world' extortion rackets, the criminal says to the local storekeeper (or whoever): 'Pay us x amount a month or the shop gets burned down.' In the botnet world the conversation is along the lines of: 'Pay us x amount or we'll take down your website.' Now, for any business, going offline is bad. But if you are, for example, an online betting company or any form of uniquely online business, any time lost online is potentially disastrous. Thus one of the favourite targets of botnet extortion attacks has been online businesses such as betting firms.

▲ Visualization of a botnet

▶ Botnets and spam

However, the botnets and DDoS attacks are not just used for straightforward extortion rackets. They can be used for political or 'cyber war' reasons to attack certain commercial websites, institutions or government departments. The botnet is, after all, simply a tool to commit cyber crime and can be used for a variety of purposes, more or less sophisticated. Sometimes these DDoS attacks are used as a diversionary technique to draw attention from other forms of attack, such as hacking, against the real target. Nor are botnets, which have become the bedrock tool of cyber crime, used only for carrying out DDoS attacks. They are often employed, for example, to send out spam messages, to harvest data to be used to commit identity theft, and to commit online advertising fraud (by infecting a browser to change what the user sees and favouring certain ads and pop-ups). Indeed, botnets are responsible for vast amounts of spam, using the email address books of their infected 'host' computers to send huge numbers of spam messages across the Internet.

An example of just how big an impact botnets have on spam and web traffic can be seen from the 2008 demise of the so-called McColo web-hosting service provider. This service provider was set up by a 19-year-old Russian student and hacker and many of the world's botnets were using its servers. These included the botnet Srizbi, said to be the world's largest botnet at the time and which was reportedly able to send up to 60 billion spam emails a day. If true, that would have been more than half of the estimated 100 billion daily spam messages sent at the time. Little wonder that McColo was described as 'biggest malicious data centre in the history of the Internet' by one observer.

McColo was shut down in November 2008 by two server suppliers that McColo used (known in the jargon as 'upstream suppliers' – the Web works on a hierarchy of servers). The immediate effect of this service provider being taken offline was swift and dramatic. Reports vary, and one cannot be sure of the precise figures, but we can say that for a period the number of spam messages being sent around the world fell by up to 80 per cent. But only for a period. Within months spam traffic flows were back close to 'normal' as new 'bot herds' were created and hosted and old ones dusted down for business.

▶ The fightback against botnets

We can understand, then, why the botnet is seen as the big beast of the World Wide Web jungle and the one that most scares heavyweights of computer security. Botnet attacks do not just bring down individual websites; they can, in theory, bring down the Internet itself, even if in practice the structures of the global network are likely to withstand even sustained attacks. The potential threat comes from botnet attacks on a key infrastructure underpinning the Internet, the domain name system (DNS) root server networks, or 'clusters'. There are

13 of these clusters in all and they are critical to the working of the Internet. On various occasions these have come under sustained DDoS attacks, though as yet little widespread disruption has been caused.

The danger posed by botnets has led to a concerted campaign against them by governments, security firms and large corporations. Botnet activity is now monitored through the use of massive resources and in a similar way to how earthquake activity is watched. Sophisticated 'listening' devices are placed in the Internet that filter Internet activity and traffic and look for early signs of bot activity. Large organizations such as telecoms operator BT and IT security firm Symantec then model the activity in control centres and show the spread of a botnet attack.

Interestingly, one of the key figures in the major fightback against botnets is Microsoft. In recent years the giant software manufacturer has devoted a great deal of time, effort and money to attacking and destroying botnets. The US multinational has set up what it has called Project Microsoft Active Response for Security (MARS), of which the avowed aim is to 'annihilate botnets and help make the Internet safer for everyone'.

This fightback against botnets has seen some success. For example, Microsoft, working as part of a team with security experts, law enforcement agencies and academics, helped close down the Rustock botnet in 2011. This was said to have taken over more than 2 million computers. An even bigger success was the joint operation involving the Canadian IT security company Defense Intelligence, Spanish IT security firm Panda Security and the Georgia Tech Information Security Center (GTISC) from the United States, against the botnet Mariposa in December 2009. This was estimated to have up to 12 million computers in its herd.

The main reason for the successes in the fight against botnets is down to co-operation, imaginative use of the law, and making the use of botnets far less profitable for their owners. Domains and servers from which they operate have been taken down or taken over. The civil law has been used to persuade courts to help the botnet-fighters in their task. For example, in their legal fight against Rustok, Microsoft argued that the botnet was abusing the firm's trade marks in its spam.

However, just as the authorities keep varying their strategy and their technology, so, too, do the criminals. Many botnet creators, for example, do not use their own 'herds' for attacks or spam. Instead, they rent them out to others, rather like guns for hire. This allows the creators of those botnets to remain one step removed from direct criminal acts. It has already proved remarkably difficult to track down and prosecute the so-called 'bot herders'. They also evolve and adapt quickly to new technology platforms. One of the most recent changes of tactics used by bot herders is to deploy botnets on smartphones.

▶ Other uses of botnets

As mentioned earlier, it is not only criminals interested in money who use botnets. So-called political hackers, or 'hactivists', use them to launch DDoS attacks against websites of institutions whose activities they oppose. One group which has used them is Anonymous. In early 2013 this hacking collective even petitioned the US government to recognize DDoS attacks as a legitimate form of protest. Other groups have used botnets to launch DDoS attacks on whole-country infrastructures, as shall be seen in Chapter 10.

7

Cyber criminal profiles

Without cyber criminals there would, of course, be no cyber crime. But the term 'cyber criminal' covers a wide range of offenders who often have very different motivations for what they do. Some do it for glory, some for politics, others for patriotic reasons – while the majority, it is true, are in it for the money. For the sake of convenience, we will split them three main categories, though within these categories there are also subgroups.

▶ Ideological hackers

In many ways, these are the most interesting of all cyber 'criminals'. The reason why one is tempted to put the word 'criminal' in inverted commas is that when telecommunications hacking began, back in the 1960s, it was not in itself a criminal offence. Simply entering a computer or telephone network – as we saw in an earlier chapter, early hacks were on phone systems – was not against the law, even though using information gathered in this way to commit offences was. It was only in the 1980s in the Western world that what might be termed 'pure' hacking was made a criminal offence.

This transition from non-criminal to the criminal is crucial and highlights an uneasy faultline that still runs through the world of computers, the Internet and the World Wide Web. For many bright young students in the 1960s, 1970s and 1980s, computers and later the Internet symbolized intellectual liberty and the free movement of information. Such views broadly coincided with a left-wing or anarchist dislike of business and commercialization. For these students, criminalizing hacking went completely against their beliefs. How could they be criminals when they were simply hacking the things they loved – computers and networks?

This approach has been passed down to successive generations of technologically minded youths. In time, many of the original young libertarians and ideologues began to realize that, as well as being fun, there was money, serious money, to be made in new technology. But this did not mean that they abandoned all those youthful beliefs. And within the academic world and on the fringes of mainstream technology, there are still unreconstructed libertarian ideologues who rail against the commercialization of the Web, the restrictions on access to information and, of course, the criminalization of hacking.

A couple of well-known examples help illustrate these continuing tensions. Bill Gates 'hacked' as a student to gain more computer time (in the days when time on computers was scarce and precious) and was certainly part of the youthful pioneering generation that underpinned the development of the computer. But Gates also had an exceptional business brain and he and his friend Paul Allen created Microsoft in 1975, which as we know has become a huge corporation. Microsoft's success and its approach to software – copyrighting its code – was anathema to many in the world of computers and technology, and still is. For them, Gates is a sell-out and Microsoft is part of the establishment.

Contrast this with the example of Steve Wozniak, the co-founder of Apple. Wozniak, too, was an early hacker, and Apple, like Microsoft, went on to become a major corporation and a big part of the modern consumer scene. Yet, to a great extent, Wozniak has retained much of the 'street credibility' that Gates does not have. This is perhaps because Wozniak has been good at managing a delicate balancing act – wanting to be part of the modern computer technology 'priesthood' for the intellectual kudos, but also wanting some of the cash. It may also help that 'Woz' stopped being a full-time employee of Apple back in 1987.

Richard Stallman

Perhaps the best example of the libertarian streak in modern technology is represented by Richard Stallman. A brilliant Harvard student, Stallman was later part of the Massachusetts Institute of Technology hacker culture and developed a lifelong belief in the freedom to use, study, distribute and modify software. In 1979 he famously described an attempt to restrict unlicensed access to a particular software as a 'crime against humanity'. In 1983 he set up the GNU Project to promote freely available software that can be distributed and modified by users.

There is, in short, a group of libertarian and mostly left-wing intellectuals involved in the world of technology whose power and influence have never really been documented. The influence of this group is profound – as is its ability to disrupt. It has members in every major university and plays a key part of the thinking of the pure hacking community. In institutional terms, the libertarian approach to the Internet and computer is broadly reflected in organizations such as Privacy International, the Electronic Privacy Information Center and the Electronic Frontier Foundation.

Today, the emergence of so-called 'hactivism', or hacking with a political motive, has shown where certain ideological descendants of the original hackers have decided to position themselves – by breaking the law for what they see as justified, non-self-serving reasons. Of the various groups that are currently operating – and they are constantly evolving, disappearing and then re-emerging – two well-known ones are Anonymous and Lulzsec. Both groups have been prominent in attacking and hacking websites of companies and organizations of which they disapprove. These have included the Church of Scientology, child pornography sites, the United Department of Justice, the FBI, the Pentagon, the Ugandan government, the Syrian government, the *Sun* newspaper in the United Kingdom and many others.

Their motivation appears to be a mixture of the mischievous and high-minded idealism. In 2012 a reporter from *The Guardian* newspaper in Britain communicated – via the Internet – with a teenage Anonymous activist who had been arrested, though not charged, with many offences. He admitted to causing a lot of damage and putting millions of people at risk of identity theft by leaking their passwords. He said such actions were never justified. When asked why in that case he had done it, the youth replied: 'At the time, it seemed great fun.'

The same newspaper also interviewed Jake Davis, then 19, who had briefly been one of the public (if anonymous) voices of the Anonymous offshoot hactivist group LulzSec. After his arrest by British police, Davis, who lived on a Scottish island, said of his time with the hactivist group that living in the Shetlands he didn't appreciate the impact of what they were doing or its impact on the real world. The impression given was of an isolated teenager finding friends online and then getting overwhelmed by what he had become involved in.

Yet there is clearly a more intellectual and committed side to groups such as Anonymous and Lulzsec. In February 2012, for example, the group gave notice that it would launch an attack on the DNS root name servers that underpin the Internet, with the aim of 'temporarily shutting it down'. It was a protest, said Anonymous, against the 'SOPA [Stop Online Piracy Act], Wallstreet [sic], our irresponsible leaders and the beloved bankers who are starving the world for their own selfish needs out of sheer sadistic fun.' Ultimately, however, the attack failed to cause any significant problems for the Internet.

As already mentioned, the same group in January 2013 petitioned the US authorities to make DDoS attacks a form of legal protest. Such attacks, argued the group, are not hacking. 'It is the equivalent of repeatedly hitting the refresh button on a web page,' it insisted. 'It is, in that way, no different than any 'occupy' protest. Instead of a group of people standing outside a building to occupy the area, they are having their computer occupy a website to slow (or deny) service of that particular website for a short time.'

Whatever one thinks of the merits of the Anonymous argument, their petition has echoes of the old idealism that infused the world of computers and software in the 1960s and 1970s. But it is precisely because groups such as Anonymous and others feel they have right on their side that some security experts and government agency officials feel that they are potentially the most dangerous kind of hacker.

▶ Cyber spies

If ideological hackers are motivated by their conscience, cyber spies work out of patriotism or simply because they are on their government's payroll. Espionage, intelligence gathering and analysis are nothing new. But since the arrival of what we might term the age of 'Information Warfare' and the massive dependence of modern societies on digital systems to keep the lights, water and most modern conveniences on, the cyber spy has become an indispensable asset to any government. These spies – whose main qualification is their ability with computers or writing software – do not just seek to spy on other governments. As we saw in Chapter 4, they also take part in industrial espionage on a grand and global scale.

Almost by definition, we do not know a great deal about the individual cyber spies employed by governments. Their time is spent quietly behind closed doors, putting endless hours into tracking threats, plotting attacks or pinpointing potential victims. This is particularly true in China, which is accused of – something it strongly denies – employing large numbers of hackers, either directly or indirectly through state-owned companies.

The West also has its cyber spies although, increasingly, Western nations are more open about them. For example, in the United States the University of Tulsa offers a two-year course in cyber spying. Students, who are taught how to write computer viruses, hack networks, crack passwords and retrieve data from different types of digital devices, are often later recruited by the National Security Agency or the CIA. The university's website reveals that it has received nearly $15 million from the National Science Foundation since 2001 for its 'Cyber Corps Program'. It quotes Dickie George, technical director of information assurance at the United States National Security Agency, as saying: 'What we need today are elite cyber warriors, and that's what this program produces.'

Applicants to the course have ranged widely in age, from 17 to 63. They also come from different backgrounds. A significant number are military veterans while some others are professionals looking for a second career. Similar courses are held at Dakota State University in South Dakota, Northeastern University in Boston and the Naval Postgraduate School in California.

The United Kingdom, too, has a relatively open policy on recruiting cyber spies. In October 2012 the British Foreign Secretary William Hague announced that De Montfort University in Leicester would be training a new generation of cyber spies to work for the country's intelligence services, including the GCHQ spy communications centre in Cheltenham and the overseas intelligence agency MI6. The aim of the scheme was described as being to tap into the so-called 'Xbox generation' who grew up in an online world. Symbolically, Hague made the announcement at Bletchley Park, the home of the Second World War code-breakers. 'It will be the young innovators of this generation who will help keep our country safe in years to come against threats which are every bit as serious as some of those confronted in the Second World War,' said the Foreign Secretary.

In addition to courses for potential cyber spies, intelligence agencies in the West monitor any young people who attract their attention through exceptional skill with computers, software and the Web. There are two reasons why the Western agencies do this. One is that these youngsters may choose to use their great technical skills for dishonest ends, or be approached by criminals and end up moving to the 'dark side'. Another is that this is a form of talent scouting – able young computer whizz kids may be recruited by the security services.

Of existing cyber spies, some of the best ones are veteran hackers from the pre-criminal days. Many of these are quite exceptionally clever, spending their time between working in academia and for private security firms and government agencies. Although it is hard to generalize, based on the authors' experiences and interviews, today's cyber spies are typically highly intelligent from backgrounds that cross the social range. There is also anecdotal evidence suggesting that a higher proportion of hackers than in the public at large has Asperger syndrome or other form of autism.

▶ Career criminals

In the Information Age, access to digital information and technology is the gateway to making money. So it is unsurprising that criminals eventually caught on to the idea that computers and the Internet provide useful tools for making serious cash. It is there, after all, that all our valuable data is stored.

There are many different types of criminal who become involved in cyber crime. There are loners or criminals working in small teams, perhaps committing credit card fraud or identity theft using both online and 'real world' techniques. There are also criminal gangs who specialize in other areas – drugs, prostitution or gun-running for example – but who may use cyber crime techniques from time to time on an ad hoc basis. For example, they may use the services of a hacker to monitor the computer/online activities of an associate or victim.

However, this section is mainly concerned with the 'full-time' cyber criminals, who broadly fall into three categories. The first of these are the high-level criminals. The next level down is the so-called 'script kiddies'. The third level contains the fall guys, the so-called 'mules' – the ones who often get caught and convicted.

High-level criminals

As their names suggests, they are the masterminds behind hacks, botnet attacks and other forms of cyber crimes. Typically, they will be talented hackers themselves, able to write or at least adapt their own codes and with an excellent understanding of both attack and defence techniques in relation to attacking websites, computers and networks. Many of the smarter ones write their malicious code, or 'malware', and sell it on to other criminals, who then use it for their own crimes. In the area of the Web known as the 'Deep Web', criminals gather, away from (most of) the prying eyes of law enforcement agents.

The Deep Web

The World Wide Web is huge, and much bigger than most of us think. The major search engines such as Google only index a fraction of it. There is a much larger portion of old messages, links and pages that are to all and intents and purposes 'invisible'. This part, once described as the 'Hidden Web', is now known as the 'Deep Web'. Because it is hidden, the Deep Web has become a place where cyber criminals often hang out, buying and selling data and software and swapping ideas. No one knows for sure how big the Deep Web is but it is many times larger than the so-called Surface Web.

The advantage for the high-level hackers and criminals in selling their software this way is that it leaves them one step removed from any crimes committed with it, making it highly unlikely that they will be caught. Typically, they are very intelligent, computer literate from an early age, and were often involved in low-level hacking in their youth.

Inevitably, the phenomenon of criminal hackers has led to rumours and legends. One of these is that there exists an elite level of hackers, called by some 'uber-hackers', who are sufficiently talented and cautious that they make large amounts of money, do not draw unwanted attention to themselves and do not get caught. It is difficult to estimate how many such uber-hackers there might be, given that by definition they rarely, if ever, get caught … and we cannot be sure they even exist anyway.

However, we do know that *some* high-level criminal hackers get caught. An example is Albert Gonzalez, a Cuban American who began hacking at high school and who was jailed for 20 years in 2010 in connection with hacks to steal and then resell information relating to 180 million credit and cash dispenser card numbers. It was the biggest fraud of its kind so far committed. By all accounts, Gonzalez, born in 1981, is a talented hacker. He bought his first computer at the age of 12 and by the age of 14 had apparently hacked into NASA. An associate lauded both Gonzalez's computer skills and his social engineering skills. .

Gonzalez was also a major figure in the ShadowCrew message board and forum that in the early 2000s acted as a kind of brokerage house, department store and training base for cyber criminals. Criminals from around the globe bought and sold stolen credit card details as well as learning about the latest scamming techniques and malware. Just to complicate matters further, it appears that Gonzalez became a police informant after he was first arrested, but then turned double agent – carrying out more cyber crimes while supposedly co-operating with the authorities. Gonzalez has applied to have his original guilty pleas withdrawn on the grounds that he was badly advised by his lawyers and was acting for the US Secret Service helping them to track other cyber criminals.

Script kiddies

The name 'script kiddie' is a pejorative term used to describe the many low-skilled wannabe hackers and cyber criminals who inhabit the Web. They are sometimes referred to as the vandals of the Internet. Script kiddies are typically young men – often teenagers – who have few, if any, programming skills and who for the most part use the software tools created by others to commit crimes, such as defacing websites and sending out (though rarely writing) computer viruses. Though considered the lowest form of life by the cyber crime elite, the kiddies are an essential part of the cyber crime ecosystem as they provide a ready source of foot soldiers for those engaged in cyber crime activities. In the last few years script kiddies have emerged as a more significant threat, due to the fact that they can be trained via Internet video systems such as YouTube. These training systems are now being used by cyber crime gangs to recruit 'soldiers'; some recruited teenagers have been earning around $5,000 a month. Script kiddies – who are also known as 'script bunnies' – can often be found hanging around online in the so-called Deep Web.

Cyber mules

Most criminal activities require 'bag carriers' who fetch and carry. Cyber crime is no different. For cyber criminals carrying out, for example, bank account frauds or credit card frauds, they need people to open bogus bank accounts or take physical possession of high-value goods bought with stolen cards. To reduce the risk of detection, the criminals use 'mules' – unskilled workers – to perform these tasks for them. As a result, there is a whole sub-industry in cyber crime devoted to recruiting mules in various countries. Usually, the mules, who are often students or the unemployed, are paid a commission for their work. This may be around 10 per cent of the transaction value. However, as a result of anti-money-laundering legislation, the level of transactions is usually kept quite low. In the United States the FBI has an ongoing operation to target the cyber mules in a bid to raise public awareness and stop people joining what one official describes as the 'army of mules' assisting cyber criminals to steal from businesses, schools and churches across the country.

8

Policing cyber space

In some respects, policing cyber crime is like any other form of policing. You track down the bad guys, find the evidence against them, arrest them and bring them to court. That, at least, is the theory. In practice, there are significant differences between cyber and many 'real world' crimes and some formidable obstacles to overcome for law enforcement agencies.

The most important is that cyber crime has, from the beginning and almost by definition, been global. Viruses, phishing emails, denial-of-service attacks, and hacks can all be launched from anywhere on the globe. Yet police forces are not historically global in nature. In the United States the Federal Bureau of Investigation (FBI) was set up to investigate crimes on a countrywide basis. But much law enforcement in the United States is still carried out at local level. The same is true in the United Kingdom where, historically, police forces have been based in counties and are self-contained law enforcement agencies. How can a police detective in, say, Butler, Pennsylvania, or Bury St Edmunds in Suffolk, possibly carry out an investigation on their own into a crime that may have originated in a quiet corner of Romania or China?

A related problem is the available skill set. A modern police officer is trained to deal with many situations and crimes. But tracking down cyber criminals is not one of them. Fighting cyber crime is for the most part an immensely time-consuming, technical and expensive business. It is simply unrealistic to expect local law enforcement agencies to take responsibility for solving them. Thus, given the threat posed by cyber crime to individuals, businesses, governments and the country as a whole, many countries have set up nationwide strategies for combating it, with an emphasis, too, on international co-operation with other nations' forces.

In the United Kingdom, this has led to the creation of successive bodies whose sole aim is to fight cyber crime. The latest body dedicated to this task is the new National Cyber Crime Unit (NCCU) that will sit alongside the equally new National Crime Agency (which replaces the Serious Organised Crime Agency). The NCCU is to take on many of the functions of the Police Central e-crime Unit (PCeU) that is based with the Metropolitan Police in London. This was itself a successor organization to the National High-Tech Crime Unit (NHTCU).

Alongside the police bodies, there are also groups tasked with protecting Britain and the country's infrastructure from large-scale threats. The organization in charge of this is the GCHQ spy centre based at Cheltenham, which focuses on the threat from botnets and advanced persistent threats, or APTs, on business and infrastructure (see Chapter 4), and overall to the threats against the UK economy. There is also a Joint Cyber Unit based in Corsham, Wiltshire, and another one hosted by GCHQ, though its aim is to assess and co-ordinate the UK's military cyber security attack capabilities rather than its defences. The British government has announced, meanwhile, that it is putting an extra £650 million into the fight against cyber crime.

Despite the money and structures put in place, it is still hard for law enforcement agencies on their own to tackle cyber crime. For one thing, as can be seen from the UK example, there have been so many different organizations with the remit to tackle cyber crime that inevitably there has been a lack of continuity. Amid the changes, experienced and able police officers who have become expert in tackling cyber crime have moved to the private sector. There has also been a recruitment problem at GCHQ. It has felt obliged to offer bonuses to top staff to attract new talent and to stop existing employees being tempted by salaries offered by large firms such as Google and Microsoft. And, although police officers who work in these units are now highly trained and proficient in their areas, there are relatively few of them compared with the vastness of the Internet and the growing number of cyber threats. In February 2013 Britain's spending watchdog, the National Audit Office, warned of a lack of skilled workers in fighting cyber crime in the country and reported fears that it could take up to 20 years to sort out the 'skills gap'.

In the United States, the responsibility for dealing with cyber attacks is split between different agencies. The Department of Homeland Security has the primary responsibility for protecting America's federal civilian networks – which means the country's infrastructure and utilities – from cyber attack. However, the organization in charge of safeguarding the country's military networks is the US Cyber Command (USCYBERCOM). This organization is currently headed by General Keith B. Alexander, who is also the head of the National Security Agency (NSA), the intelligence agency that gathers and analyses information from foreign communications.

The National Security Agency

The National Security Agency has a key role to play in fighting cyber attacks, as it now has responsibility for protecting US government communications and information systems. In 2008 the agency was given this wider role when it was authorized to monitor the computer networks of all federal agencies. In recent years the NSA has also stepped up its recruitment campaign to attract new 'cyber professionals'. Its website has a section devoted to attracting new talent, in which it states: 'At NSA, knowing cyberspace matters... Apply today for a position with NSA as a cyber professional, and enjoy an exciting career within the dynamic, fast-paced world of cyberspace.'

As well as the Department of Homeland Security, US Cyber Command and the NSA, the CIA and the FBI also have a role in fighting cyber attacks. The latter has its own well-funded Cyber Division that has, since 2011, stepped up its efforts to produce a 'cadre of specially trained computer scientists able to extract hackers' digital signatures from mountains of malicious code'. Its agents have also been developing links with cyber security experts in the private sector, whose job it is to protect the infrastructures for finance, business, transport and other key sectors.

The FBI points out that its Cyber Division's Cyber Watch command post shares the information it receives with the other agencies, such as Departments of Defense and Homeland Security and the National Security Agency. This is done via yet another organization, the National Cyber Investigative Joint Task Force, which is led by the FBI itself and which brings together 18 intelligence and law enforcement agencies. Set up in 2007, a year later it was officially designated as the 'focal point for all government agencies to co-ordinate, integrate, and share information related to all domestic cyber threat investigations'. Despite the task force's work, there are some concerns that the presence of so many agencies in the cyber crime arena can lead to confusion, rivalries and turf wars, although the NSA is generally seen as the lead agency in tackling cyber crime.

▶ Private crime fighters

Despite the presence of an increasing number of highly trained law enforcement officers around the world, on their own they do not have the capability to tackle cyber crime. The Internet is so vast and so concentrated in the hands of private companies; the dependence of so much of the world's critical infrastructure is so great, and the work so complex and technical, that it is simply not possible. This is why, in contrast to many other areas of crime, the private sector has a major role in fighting online crime. In a sense, it is a return to the Wild West of the second half of the 19th century, when there were private agencies such as the Pinkerton Detective Agency patrolling remote lawless areas of the United States.

Today we have private computer security firms who monitor the Internet looking for signs of attack, from viruses or botnets, and who venture into the darkest reaches of the Deep Web looking for trends in criminal activity. In many cases, firms such as Kapersky, Symantec, McAfee and

Trend Micro have become household names. Some have major operation centres in which expert analysts minutely observe the flow of traffic on the Internet, 24 hours a day, every day, watching for signs of botnet attacks massing or the evolution of viruses. If there is a war against cyber crime, then these are the operations rooms, with their futuristic screens and displays.

Such firms typically make their revenue from selling antivirus (AV) and other software to consumers and providing bespoke cyber security solutions for larger companies and governments. But, as part of their wider services, they also produce regular reports on likely threats and trends in cyber crime activity. In so doing, they perform an important function, not just for the police and other law enforcement and intelligence agencies, but for government, businesses and consumers. They are, therefore, an important part of the network of agencies that combat cyber crime.

The world of academia also plays an important role in the fight against cyber crime. We have already seen how institutions in the United States and the United Kingdom are training the 'cyber spies' of tomorrow to fight online threats. But a number of universities also have top academic computer and Internet experts who are able to provide detailed forensic and analytical skills that are vital to law enforcement agencies. In the United Kingdom, departments at Bristol, Lancaster, Royal Holloway College, Imperial College, University College London, Queen's University Belfast, Southampton, Oxford, the University of South Wales, De Montfort, York, Edinburgh and Glasgow all carry out work on behalf of law enforcement agencies.

Facebook fights back

Increasingly, technology companies are taking the lead in fighting back against the hackers and other criminals who attack their sites and networks. When in 2010 Facebook came under concerted attack from malicious software, it decided to take the initiative and start investigating the hackers rather than just defending itself against the attacks. As Facebook's security researcher Mark Hammel told the media: 'We're not happy playing the whack-a-mole game.' Thanks to the social media network's help, in 2012 the FBI was able to announce that the authorities had arrested ten members of an international cyber crime ring.

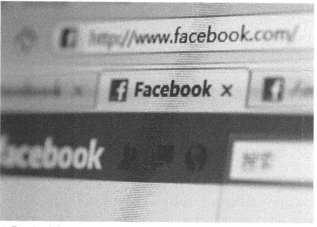

▲ Facebook is no stranger to cyber attacks but in more recent years has gone on the offensive, by helping to track down hackers.

Inevitably, too, public utilities are involved in the fight against cyber crime. At the forefront in Britain is BT, the telecommunications giant, which owns much of the physical network – the telephone lines and fibre-optic cable – through which the Internet runs. The company has, for example, a contract with Britain's Ministry of Defence to safeguard its IT network and is a member of the UK government's joint task force on cyber defence, the UK Cyber Hub initiative. But other key industries such as water, oil, gas and electricity also have significant cyber defence capability and employ experts to protect these key assets from attacks.

The interrelated nature of cyber security protection in the United Kingdom – as elsewhere – is underlined by the emphasis on 'public–private partnership' – that is, a sharing of information, ideas and expertise. This is in recognition of the fact that a key part of the country's economy is now in the hands of private companies such as phone operators and Internet service providers. This important area, the crossover between the private and public infrastructures that govern our lives, is handled by the Centre for the Protection of National Infrastructure (CPNI). Its primary aim is to ensure that key sectors such as water, energy, health and the communications networks are as well protected as they can be against all forms of attack, including cyber attacks.

9

Targeting children

The Internet is of enormous benefit to children, for their education and their development. However, at the same time it has exposed young people to greater potential risks than ever before. At the press of a button they can access the murkiest reaches of the Web from their own bedroom. Understandably, then, parents are anxious to ensure that children are as safe online as they can be. However, as we shall see in this chapter, children are not only the potential victims of cyber crime, they can be its unwitting allies, too. Any defence system is only as strong as its weakest point, and when it comes to defending our computers, networks and private information, unfortunately the natural curiosity and impetuosity of youngsters can make them a weak link.

▶ Paedophilia

First, however, we need to consider a subject that generates more lurid headlines and causes more concern in society than any other aspect of cyber crime – paedophilia. The abuse of children and the taking of photographs and films of the abuse of children are clearly nothing new. What has changed is the extent to which paedophile images have been made widely available because of the Internet, and the way that organized paedophile groups can communicate over long distances in secrecy.

The point about the easy availability of paedophile images is an important one. The fact that paedophile sites are so easily accessible via a computer has undoubtedly led to many more people being 'tempted' to view them than was previously the case. Whether this has led to a greater number of paedophiles per se is a complex and controversial question. One can, for example, draw a distinction between the hardcore 'abuser' on the one hand and the 'user' or viewer of graphic images on the other. The latter group has certainly increased in number since the arrival of the Internet. Certain experts, however, maintain that such exposure to images may lead some – or even many – into becoming more 'active' paedophiles.

Criminals are usually quick to adopt technological breakthroughs, and paedophiles are no different. Back in 1989 one of the authors of this book, Peter Warren, was involved in an investigation that revealed how paedophiles had started to use a brand-new chat room system to swap explicit images with one another. The matter prompted the Greater Manchester Police in north-west England to start investigations into online pornography, the first occasion that the British police undertook such a project.

An even more serious example of paedophiles embracing new techniques came in the mid-2000s. During the course of the police operation Project Wickerman, detectives uncovered a worldwide paedophile ring that originated in Canada but whose control had been passed to the United Kingdom. The hundreds of members of this highly secretive ring communicated via a file-sharing service. At the time, the potential for the criminal exploitation of such file-sharing sites was not fully appreciated. The ring members were linked together by the site, which they used to exchange images of abuse they had carried out on their own children and children that they had access to, often producing porn movies on demand for other members of the ring.

An arrest in Canada gave detectives entry to the chat rooms in question and computer experts then broke the encryption mechanism used on the file-sharing system. Once inside the chat rooms, the officers were able to watch the ring's members exchange tips on Internet and computer security. Law and order agencies from no fewer than 35 countries were involved in Project Wickerman, which led to a string of convictions in 2007.

▶ Operations Avalanche and Ore

Perhaps the most infamous of such paedophile rings led to the international police investigation known as Operation Avalanche. This followed a raid on a pornography portal website based in Texas in the United States that had links to a number of child abuse websites, and which provided online payment services for some of them. FBI agents discovered around 35,000 names of 'subscribers' on the Texan company's books, scattered in many nations around the world. The information was shared with law enforcement agencies in those countries and resulted in a number of high-profile follow-on investigations. These included Operation

Amethyst in Ireland, Operation Pecunia in Germany, Operation Snowball in Canada and Operation Genesis in Switzerland. In the United Kingdom the resulting investigation was called Operation Ore.

Operation Ore began in 2002 after the FBI handed over the names and addresses of 7,272 Britons who had apparently bought images depicting child abuse via the Texan site's payment service. By the time prosecutions had been concluded, some 1,837 convictions had been secured and 710 cautions handed out, according to the Child Exploitation and Online Protection Centre (CEOP), the body set up in 2006 to bring online child sex offenders to court.

What was striking about Operation Ore was that many of the people arrested and many of those subsequently convicted were men who had never previously come to the attention of law enforcement agencies as actual or potential child sex offenders.

'Celebrities' caught up in Operation Ore

Among the men caught up in Operation Ore were some high-profile names. The former The Who guitarist Pete Townshend was given a police caution in 2003 after admitting to Operation Ore detectives that he had visited a child pornography website. However, the police accept that he never downloaded an image and Townshend says that he was researching a book. Then, in 2007, the British actor Chris Langham was convicted of downloading child pornography and given a ten-month jail sentence, reduced to six months on appeal.

Operation Ore caused considerable controversy. One issue was that a number of entirely innocent people were pursued by the authorities, as their credit cards had been stolen or cloned – copied – to make payments on the Texan portal. For example, a businessman, Jeremy Clifford, from Watford in south-east England, successfully sued his local police force for malicious prosecution after he was investigated for allegedly downloading ten images – though the prosecution dropped the criminal case before it went to court. In another example, charges against the pop musician Robert Del Naja from the band Massive Attack were dropped in March 2003 after it emerged that his credit card details had been stolen and used to make a payment at the Texan website. One cyber crime had been used to commit another.

Another issue was that the sheer scale of Operation Ore swamped the British police at the very time that other forms of cyber crime – such as online identity theft – were beginning to become more widespread. Police resources for computer-related investigations became largely focused on Operation Ore, which in some police forces created backlogs of more than two years. There is little doubt that a number of other cyber crimes at the time received less or even no investigation time because of the focus on Operation Ore.

However, the authorities in Britain point out that, of more than 2,400 people who were 'successfully held to account' – convicted or cautioned – 93 per cent had admitted their guilt. And one clear consequence of the huge publicity accorded to Operation Ore was a reduction in the number of people going to such websites.

One could say since Operation Ore the 'casual market' for paedophile images appears to have been discouraged.

One of the disturbing lessons learned from the above cases was the realization that criminal gangs had muscled in on what has become a hugely lucrative 'business'. One study has put the trade in paedophile images at $3 billion annually. According to Ernie Allen, the executive director of the United States' National Center for Missing and Exploited Children, the reality of the Internet is that child porn images have become a commodity. For organized crime, it is easier to make money from exploiting child abuse than from other traditional sources of income. 'Children are plentiful and there is easy access,' he told a conference in Washington in December 2006. 'There's basically no risk, unlike with drugs and guns. When organized crime understands that there is money to be made they don't care what the product is,' he said.

Allen has said that if the authorities 'choke the money ... you choke the supply'. And it is certainly true that a concerted effort by bodies such as the National Center for Missing and Exploited Children has led to a huge reduction in the use of credit cards for online transactions involving images of child abuse. However, other forms of payment processes have often been used as alternatives, and it has also proved difficult for law enforcement agencies to get the full co-operation of banks in areas where many of the criminal gangs operating child porn sites are based.

▶ Social networks and grooming

A major concern for all parents is the risk of their child being approached by potential abusers online. The practice of abusers befriending youngsters – often by concealing their real age and identity – in order to gain their trust is known as 'grooming'. This practice exists in the offline world, too, but the anonymity of chat rooms and message boards has made the Internet a favourite operating zone for child abusers. Precise figures are hard to come by, but in the mid-2000s the US Department of Justice estimated that one in five young Internet users receive an unwanted online sexual advance. At the same time, the National Center for Missing and Exploited Children said its CyberTipline had

▲ The Internet offers children an unparalleled opportunity for learning but it also makes them vulnerable to criminals.

received information on more than 16,000 cases of online enticement of children for sexual acts since 1998.

No need for 'grooming'

There is disturbing evidence that abusers do not even need to take the trouble to 'groom' children any more. An in-depth study of abuser behaviour by Kingston University and the National Centre for Social Research in the United Kingdom for the European Online Grooming Project, published in 2012, found that paedophiles' online chats turned sexual within just two minutes. Professor Julia Davidson of Kingston University, one of the study's authors, said: 'On social networking sites, if the child does not respond, the offender will simply move on to the next child. During our interviews, offenders said they didn't need to bother with a grooming process when they could immediately ask children for sex or to meet so they could abuse them.'

▶ The security risks caused by children

Children are not just potential victims online. They can also present a possible risk for their families and schools. At different times young people can be naive, pliant, gullible, impetuous, subversive and mischievous. Thus, for all the reasons that young people are attractive to society at large, they are attractive to the denizens of the dark side of the Web. They also possess one even more compelling attraction for the criminal – they can be easily manipulated.

According to Tim Wilson of the information technology security organization ISC2, who teaches cyber awareness courses in the south-east of England, in every class of children that he takes, someone can recount an incident where they have infected a home PC. Wilson, a former police officer, says that parents have often lost significant amounts of money from their bank accounts due to such incidents. Wilson relates how, in one case, a parent lost £10,000.

In particular, youngsters tend not to appreciate that the currency of the Internet is information. The result is that children are often prepared to exchange information for free things. And there are plenty of opportunities to do this. On 1 November 2012 research by the computer company Bit9 revealed that more than 100,000 Android downloadable applications or 'apps' in the Google Play store (which does not insist that apps are checked before they are offered for sale) are 'suspicious' or 'questionable'. Twenty-six per cent of these apps could access users' personal data, including contacts and email addresses.

Youngsters are also willing to go to the more dangerous places on the Internet while looking for what used to be known in the fringe community of hacking as 'wares' or 'warez'. These are simply products that are offered for free to those willing to download them. They are computer games, music files, DVDs and so on that have been 'cracked' – essentially illegal copies that can be opened with a registration code that has been posted on a site. Young computer users often learn about the sites where such programs are hosted almost as soon as they know about the Internet.

However, it would be entirely wrong to blame the youngsters alone. Many families simply ignore the basic rules of online security and do not use the software programs available to protect home networks. If parents cannot be bothered to take Internet security seriously, then their children can hardly be expected to do so.

10

Cyber warfare and the information war

The face of warfare changed in November 2010. This was when the Iranian president Mahmoud Ahmadinejad admitted that his country's uranium enrichment plant at Natanz had been damaged by a computer virus apparently specifically designed to disrupt the facility. The virus was called Stuxnet, and the confirmation that it had been used to attack a nuclear plant sent shock waves around the world. While the general public was amazed at the audacity and high-tech nature of the attack, experts realized that a page had been turned in the story of warfare. The arms race between competing powers in the world was no longer just about who had the biggest rockets, the most tanks or the fastest jets. It was also about who could produce the most effective 'weaponized software', to launch cyber attacks on the enemy.

There has been much speculation about who had created Stuxnet and used it to attack Iran's nuclear programme, with the United States and Israel regarded as the most likely culprits. But, for the purposes of this book, who sent it is less important than why it was sent – and its implications for modern-day warfare. We have become used to the way that 'traditional' war is carried out: aerial bombardment followed by tanks and boots on the ground. But this new kind of war – like the traditional kind – is still just a means to an end, to bring an enemy country to its knees (and usually the negotiating table).

What the use of Stuxnet showed is what has been apparent to experts for some years – that there are cheaper, more effective and less bloody ways of waging war on other nations. The attack on Iran involved a nuclear facility because that is the issue – Iran's potential

Image Credit: Digital Globe - ISIS
Image Date: 2 January 2006

Approximate location
of underground
cascade halls for the
Fuel Enrichment Plant

Hidden entrance
to underground
facilities

Location of the
Pilot Fuel Enrichment
Plant

★ = New construction

▲ US surveillance image of Natanz, the Iranian nuclear facility that was the target of the Stuxnet cyber attack in 2010

to build a nuclear bomb – that has placed it in conflict with much of the Western world. But a similar virus could work just as well on all other kinds of facilities and infrastructures. Nowadays a country's so-called 'critical infrastructure' – water reservoir and pumping systems, power grids, telecommunications networks and a host of other critical parts of modern-day life – all depend on computers, digital chips and automated systems to make them work. This has made them far more efficient and cost-effective to run, but it has also left them vulnerable. Taking out a country's ability to function, and thus crippling its economy and its people's lifestyle within a very short timeframe, is now a real possibility – and an alternative to conventional warfare.

Before Stuxnet, we had all known that computer viruses and other forms of malware were a real nuisance and often had an economic cost. But the realization that a virus could in fact take down a nuclear plant – and perhaps a power grid or water network, too – has changed our thinking. As one researcher into the Stuxnet virus told the authors at the time of the Iranian incident: 'The consequences of making a computer virus that works with an industrial device raises their significance by an order of magnitude. You could have watched a film like *Die Hard 4* and thought "No, that would have never have happened". Now, you think "Maybe it could."' Another impact of Stuxnet was that it had tremendous propaganda value, as it demonstrated intellectual and technological superiority.

▶ Cyber attacks and water services

In March 2000, on Queensland's Sunshine Coast, Australia, the newly built water supply and sewage system at Maroochy Water Services suddenly shut down. Investigations showed the cause had to be external. The hacker turned out to be a former contractor, Vitek Boden, who had originally installed the system. The local council had not hired Boden as a full-time employee and so, using a laptop and wireless equipment, he attacked the system, perhaps hoping to be called in to fix the problem. Instead, he ended up in jail, but not before showing the vulnerability of such systems to outside attack.

Some may still find the idea that an entire country could be vulnerable to cyber attack a little far-fetched. However, in a sense it has already happened. In 2007 the Baltic country of Estonia came under a sustained cyber attack that began on 27 April and lasted into the middle of May. Websites belonging to many of the country's leading organizations such as government ministries, broadcasters, newspapers, banks and the nation's parliament were subjected to persistent distributed denial-of-service (DDoS) attacks (see Chapter 6), launched with the aid of botnets. Although the country was not quite 'taken offline', the sustained and sophisticated attack did cause widespread disruption to websites and online services.

Inevitably, questions were raised as to who carried out the attacks – and why. Suspicion pointed to Russian involvement because the two countries were at the time involved in a heated dispute about the moving of a Soviet-era commemorative statue to Second World War war dead in Tallinn. The Estonian foreign minister blamed Russia. However, Moscow vehemently denied any involvement.

This was not, however, the end of such cyber attacks. In August 2008 the government in Georgia launched a conventional military attack to regain parts of the South Ossetia region that it claimed as part of its territory.

Russia responded by deploying forces to defend its South Ossetian allies. At the same time, Georgian websites and networks, including government and military and financial networks, came under sustained DDoS attacks. Interestingly, the attackers also took down a well-known Georgian hacking forum, possibly as a pre-emptive strike to stop Georgian hackers retaliating. The cyber assaults were so severe that Georgia needed the help of nearby allies such as Poland to keep key websites online. It was the first recorded case of a cyber attack on a country coinciding with a 'real world' military attack and thus, just possibly, the blueprint for future conflicts.

Once again, the Russians were suspected of being behind the cyber attack and, once again, they denied it. However, as some pointed out at the time, who else would have benefited? Analysts also pointed out that the cyber attacks appeared to be co-ordinated with the military action, suggesting at least some level of co-operation between the cyber attackers and the Russian authorities. Georgian authorities certainly blamed the Russians for the strikes. However, it is notoriously hard to pinpoint where such attacks come from, as they can be routed from far-distant servers to disguise their origins.

It seems unlikely that the Russian government itself was wholly responsible for either of the two cyber attack episodes, although, equally, it is hard to believe that it was not involved in at least some degree of co-ordination, certainly in the Georgian episode. What we are probably left with, instead, is the involvement of hacker or cyber 'militias'. It has been speculated for some time that states have been developing hacking armies, and the Estonian and Georgian attacks may be examples where these semi-autonomous groups have been put to use. At the time of the Georgian cyber assault there was a mass 'nationalization' of the Russian hacking websites, which were suddenly decked in Russian flags. Using militia groups has an advantage as it gives states 'deniability'. This may not fool most observers, who can have a good guess as to who is behind an attack, but in diplomacy such deniability has its uses.

General Sun Tzu

One of the gurus of Information Warfare is the Chinese general Sun Tzu who died about 2,500 years ago. His work *The Art of War* has been taught at the US National Defense University and the UK's Defence Intelligence School in Chicksands. The general's thin volume of thoughts has been carried by many of those who consider themselves thinkers and 'thought-leaders' in IT. Among the general's adages are 'If you know both yourself and your enemy, you can win numerous battles without jeopardy' and 'All warfare is based on deception.'

Another famous cyber attack on a country, albeit of a slightly different nature, involved the United States as the victim. For two years from 2003, waves of co-ordinated assaults hit US military and other key networks. The motivation behind these advanced and persistent threats – which were given the name Titan Rain – appears to have been to gather sensitive data, though some experts have also suggested that the attacks were an attempt by the hackers to test their capability to penetrate sensitive networks. Given the sheer scale and sophistication of the attacks, experts have generally concluded that they were carried out with, at the very least, some form of backing from the Chinese authorities. Beijing, of course, denied any involvement.

Yet another series of attacks – given the name Moonlight Maze – hit the United States even earlier, from 1998. Once again, US military networks were the primary targets. The main 'suspects' behind these attacks were Russian groups, though the Russian government denied any involvement.

▶ Flame and other spyware

Despite all these other attacks, it was the furore created by the discovery of Stuxnet that took concern over cyber warfare to a new level. This concern was further fuelled by the emergence of 'spyware' the first example of which was a program known as Flame. Unlike Stuxnet, whose aim was to take down a nuclear plant, the Flame malware appears to have been built with the sole aim of conducting cyber espionage. It was discovered in 2012 on Iranian oil ministry computers and seems to have been largely restricted to the Middle East, with most infections taking in places in Iran, Syria, Lebanon, Saudi Arabia, Egypt and Israel. What was particularly striking was that it had been in existence for such a long time – between two and five years. Crawling slowly through the Internet, it had appeared benign and had been ignored.

Once news of Flame's existence became public, it pretty much vanished; its controllers sent out a 'kill' command to wipe it off computers.

In addition to Flame, another spyware known as 'Gauss' has also come to light. Gauss, probably deployed for the first time in 2011, is a system targeting banking systems to discover exactly how they worked, particularly banks in Lebanon. Gauss also contains an encrypted warhead, encrypted multiple times in an extremely complex way. Experts have struggled to break the code and discover the true purpose of the spyware's payload. Yet another spyware that has come to light is Red October. A key feature of this sophisticated software is that not only does it infect USB data sticks, it can un-delete old files on them. USB sticks are typically used to transfer data in embassies between secure systems and systems that are linked to the Internet. You delete the file, take it off the secure system and then move it to the Internet-linked system so that you can work and communicate via the Web. Red October can apparently un-delete files that were supposedly wiped off the stick and send copies of them back to the 'spy master'.

Spyware such as Flame has been described as arguably the most complex form of malware yet created; it is said to be many times more complicated than Stuxnet. This is some claim, because Stuxnet had a feature that has already rung alarm bells for those people responsible for maintaining their country's critical infrastructures. It did not just take down an industrial system; it also changed the system's safety settings to disguise this fact from anyone who was overseeing the process. In other words, the system showed observers that it was working normally, even while the virus was damaging it. This has enormous and worrying implications. If an attacker can get in without anyone knowing and interfere with settings, it means that one cannot rely on *any* settings. It means experts would have to examine settings across the entire infrastructure and either double-check and then lock them down or replace them.

The potential vulnerability to Stuxnet-style attacks explains why a number of political and industrial leaders have spoken out in recent years about the urgent need to protect national infrastructures. Sir Michael Rake, chairman of the British telecommunications giant BT, said at a cyber security conference in 2011: 'With the dependence we have on technology, a state could absolutely be brought to its knees without any military action whatsoever.' In the same year, the British foreign secretary William Hague made a wide-ranging speech on 'Security and Freedom in the Cyber Age'. While acknowledging the many positive changes that the Internet was bringing to society, Hague went on to say:

> But there is a darker side to cyberspace that arises from our dependence on it. We rely on computer networks for the water in our taps, the electricity in our kitchens, the 'sat navs' in our cars, the running of trains, the storing of our medical records, the availability of food in our supermarkets and the flow of money into high-street cash machines.

Yet it should not be forgotten that Stuxnet and Flame – which shared certain similarities – were probably written by expert programmers in Israel and/or the United States (two 'friendly' nations as far as the UK is concerned). Thus, it is not only Russia, China and North Korea that are developing cyber offensive capability as well as their defensive strategies. In late 2011 the British government announced that it was setting up a 'joint cyber unit' at a military facility at Corsham in southern England that will develop a 'range of new techniques, including proactive measures to disrupt threats to our information security' – in other words, cyber weapons to be used in pre-emptive strikes. A second cyber unit has been established at the British government's spy communications centre at GCHQ in Cheltenham in the west of England that will develop 'new tactics, techniques and plans to deliver military effects through operations in cyberspace'. Again, this is government-speak for making plans to carry out cyber attacks.

There are some mundane practical reasons why countries would want to develop cyber attack capability, in addition to the fact that it can be very effective. The most important one is cost. So-called 'weaponized software' is much cheaper than the hardware equivalent. It has been estimated, for example, that Stuxnet cost around the same as a cruise missile – and did far more damage to the Iranian nuclear programme than a cruise missile would have done. Yet the 'low cost of entry' in cyber warfare compared with conventional war or nuclear weapons has a serious downside, too. It has opened up the world to a number of powers who were nowhere near getting a bomb or posing a serious military threat to anyone, but who can afford a cyber weapon. Naturally, it is the more developed powers that are most vulnerable to such attacks because of their reliance on computer technology.

▶ The cyber enemy within...

As with conventional warfare, cyber warfare is not only used for attacking other nations – it can also be used for attacking your own people. One of the most notorious examples was during the Syrian civil war that began in 2011. When they were not trying to take the Internet offline, the authorities in Damascus were accused of using malware against opponents of the regime. Specifically, they embedded Trojan programs in emails and documents that purported to be helpful to the rebel cause and that were then sent to activists. The apparent aim was to take over dissident websites and social media accounts and also monitor the activists' communications.

▶ Cyber terrorism

There has been much speculation in recent years about if and when terrorists would launch cyber attacks on their enemies. So far, however, the threat has not materialized. One reason is that terrorist groups mistrust direct involvement in computer crime. This is because its global nature represents a threat to their tight-knit cell structures. There has been evidence that al-Qaeda has unsuccessfully tried to recruit computer science academics working in North African universities. So far, however, terrorist cyber activity has largely involved money laundering. For example, there is evidence that some Chechen cyber crime groups have been providing 'bullet-proof' hosting – meaning top security hosting – and also paying a proportion of their profits from cyber crime itself to Islamic terrorist groups. There have even been suggestions of Islamic groups being involved in both the hosting of paedophile websites and pornographic websites as a means of laundering drug money.

Western governments have been preparing for possible attacks from al-Qaeda-linked terrorists. The British government's cyber security strategy voices concerns that terrorists will one day use cyber weapons to attack key infrastructure such as water, power or financial systems. 'While terrorists can be expected to continue to favour high-profile physical attacks, the threat that they might also use cyberspace to facilitate or to mount attacks against the UK is growing,' it says.

11

Future technology: how the world is getting more mobile, cloudier and more dangerous

It is one of the truisms of crime that criminals always catch up with the latest technology – and often faster than the general public. The invention of cars, telephones, mobile phones, electronic pagers, message boards and websites have all been enthusiastically embraced by criminals, who have been quick to use their value as a tool or source of money.

But nowadays it is not just the tools of the criminal job that have changed – it is the immediate target, too. When asked why he robbed banks, a criminal is once said to have replied: 'Because that's where the money is.' The story may be apocryphal, but you get the idea. The equivalent criminal today might well be asked why he targets websites, to which the answer would be: 'Because that's where the information is.'

In the 'old days', money was 'stored' as banknotes and coins, and these physical entities were what criminals sought. Today the amount of accessible money in banknotes is small compared with the money that is stored in the new way – electronically. Our money is simply digits in a database. To retrieve that money we need information – name, address and passwords and so on – and this is why one of the main preoccupations of cyber criminals is getting their hands on our personal information. It is personal information that serves as the gateway for criminals to get their hands on our money.

The way we keep our personal information is changing, too. Once it was stored in filing cabinets, then perhaps on our computer at home. Now it is just as likely to be kept on a mobile phone or other portable device. Inevitably, the criminals have caught on to this trend and there are now viruses aimed specifically at mobile phones and related devices. This trend is likely to grow. Consumers have adopted the smartphone as an indispensable part of their lives; for a growing number it is their portal of choice to the Internet. One of the latest trends is to encourage people to use their phones to make payments online or in shops. There are a variety of different ways of doing this. But the key point is that important consumer information – including passwords and bank account details – will be stored on the device. Potentially, this makes them vulnerable to malware attacks. It was estimated in late 2012 that the number of people who would access their bank services from their smartphones would soon reach 530 million worldwide. The Internet security firm ESET has meanwhile forecast what it calls an 'exponential growth' in mobile malware in the near future.

Another trend that will continue is the targeting of social media sites. Sites such as Facebook have been one of the great online success stories of recent years. But they are also potential gold mines of information, where people very helpfully store their dates of birth, geographical locale, education details, partners' and children's names and so on. This explains why criminals have used viruses to target Facebook and other social media sites in the last few years. In 2012, for example, the United States' FBI arrested ten members of a suspected international cyber crime gang who had been traced with the help of Facebook's own security team (see Chapter 8). The gang is said to have infected up to 11 million computers with a virus and caused $850 million in losses. Twitter, too, has been hit by viruses and spam aimed specifically at it, although the company claims it is 'doing well on the front lines' in reducing spam levels.

▶ Among the clouds

One of the biggest trends in the Internet in recent years has been the emergence of what is known as the 'cloud' – or 'cloud computing'. The practice has been well marketed, even if some experts believe the hype is more about marketing then anything else.

The essence of the cloud involves where your data and software are stored. In the past we have usually stored our data on our computer's hard drive and downloaded software to use as we wish. In cloud computing the information and software are stored not on your computer but on a cloud service provider's own network servers. This network is in effect the 'cloud' that the user, as a client of that cloud provider, can access as they want.

There are many advantages in cloud computing for individuals and businesses alike. It can reduce costs, the cloud can be accessed easily from anywhere, and it also enables users to take advantage of the latest technologies in software that they might not otherwise use. However, from a security point of view there are potential drawbacks. In theory, having data stored with a cloud provider should be safer than storing it on a computer. Because of their scale and size, the cloud providers are able to buy the best defences against cyber attacks. The problem is that their very size – and the amount of data they have from different companies – makes them very tempting targets. For criminals, it is probably more cost and time efficient to break into one big network than hack into lots of smaller ones. And the history of crime suggests that, when criminals are determined enough to break into something, they can usually succeed. The process of taking over a cloud in this way even has its own picturesque name – 'cloud hijacking'. With so many firms now moving key data to the cloud to boost productivity and cut costs, we can expect more stories of data theft through 'cloud hijacking' in the future.

There is another issue with the cloud and security, too. Can they be used by botnets to launch attacks across the Internet? In 2012 a security company Stratsec carried out a test of five cloud providers and found that in each case they could set up botnets on them – incidentally, clouds themselves are essentially benign botnets – and start attacks with impunity. None of the cloud providers raised alerts or sought to close down the accounts that had been opened to send the 'attacks'. One can safely say that, if security firms are finding this loophole in some cloud providers, then criminals will already have done so, too.

▶ Educating the public and business

In terms of computer security, one big trend for the future is likely to be even greater emphasis on individual consumers protecting their data, computers and phones from attack. For many, perhaps most, users of the Internet, DDoS attacks, hacking and malware probably seem remote issues affecting big business and government. Relatively few realize that their computers can be taken over and become part of a botnet without them even being aware of it. Putting too much personal information in public places – such as social networks – can also leave them open to being victims of identity theft. Similarly, there will be greater emphasis, too, on the risks that employees may unwittingly pose to their companies when using personal computers and phones at work (see Chapter 4).

But it is not just employees and individuals who will need to be educated. Many businesses are surprisingly blasé about their vulnerability to cyber attack. Howard Schmidt, who was the Cyber-Security Co-ordinator for US President Barack Obama until 2012, says that one of the biggest issues is awareness. 'There are still some people out there who will say yes, that's not going to happen to me because we do things a little differently to those companies,' he told the authors. For him, the answer is better and earlier training on the issue:

> I think that we need to make sure that the business schools are teaching this to them. Those people in business need to know about financial risk, about sales risks or the international disruption of rare earth materials, perhaps, but they all need to know about cyber risks.

▶ The future of war

As we saw in the last chapter, the kind of techniques seen in cyber crime – hacking, distributed denial-of-service attacks – have been adapted for use in the new world of cyber warfare. Most attention will be on the military attack viruses such as Stuxnet and the use of co-ordinated cyber attacks such as those carried out against Georgia. The discovery of the Stuxnet and Flame viruses raised the question of whether there were more examples of such cyber warfare malware being deployed that have yet to be found. The discovery of Gauss and Red October shows that the answer is 'yes'. Many Western countries as well as countries such as Iran, North Korea, China and Russia have manpower and money devoted to developing so-called weaponized software.

As for all-out cyber attacks, we cannot expect that they will replace conventional military assaults any time in the near future. Wars between countries fought solely on the Internet still belong to science fiction and the mid to distant future. But our already huge and growing dependence on automatized infrastructure means that such assaults will form part of new military attack doctrines. The blueprint may well be similar to those seen in Georgia, with cyber attacks aimed at key military and civilian networks co-ordinated with air strikes and troops and tanks on the ground. From now on, generals will have to understand the capability of DDoS attacks, just as they currently have to understand the capability of attack helicopters or raids by special forces.

This 100 Ideas section gives ways you can explore the subject in more depth. It's much more than just the usual reading list.

100 IDEAS

Ten cyber crime websites

1   www.zdnet.com Global technology website

2   www.cybercitizenship.org/crime/crime.html
Promoting awareness of cyber crime among young people

3   www.computerweekly.com/resources/Hackers-and-cybercrime-prevention

4   www.theregister.co.uk/security/ Respected UK computer and technology magazine

5   http://cybercrime.org.za/ Cyber crime awareness portal in South Africa

6   www.ccmostwanted.com/ Cyber Criminals Most Wanted: news, views and advice

7   www.interpol.int/Crime-areas/Cybercrime/Cybercrime
The international agency Interpol also tackles cyber crime.

8 www.virusbtn.com/resources/cybercrime/index Email bulletin with news and advice on viruses

9 http://thehackernews.com/ Lively news site

10 www.net-security.org Major site dedicated to Internet security

Ten places of hacking pilgrimage

11 Bletchley Park The home of the UK establishment's code-breaking efforts against the Germans during the Second World War. Bletchley also saw the first attempt at hacking.

12 Massachusetts Institute of Technology (MIT), Cambridge, MA The place that housed the Railway Club, the world's first hacking club (legal at the time). This was a group of model railway enthusiasts who 'broke' bits of technology and 'hacked them' to make components for their train layout.

13 Stanford Research Institute, Buckinghamshire, UK The first node on the World Wide Web that was then connected to MIT to make MIT the second node and create the first Internet connection.

14 Royal Holloway University, London, UK The home of the establishment's first efforts to come to terms with issues of computer security. The Royal Holloway, thanks to Professor Fred Piper, started the science of computer security.

15 Home Brew Computer Club, Menlo Park, CA The Homebrew Computer Club was an informal group of electronics enthusiasts and technically minded hobbyists who gathered to trade parts, circuits and information pertaining to DIY construction of computing devices. It was started by Gordon French and Fred Moore who met at the Community Computer Center in Menlo Park.

16 The computer room in Cornell University, Ithaca, NY Where Robert Morris launched the first Internet worm in 1988.

17 The computer room in Lawrence Berkeley National Laboratory, CA A computer manager, Clifford Stoll, was asked to resolve a 75-cent billing error and, in doing so, discovered an intrusion by German hackers into NATO systems, later described in his book *The Cuckoo's Egg* (see below).

18 Buckingham Gate, London A brown office building houses the world's first computer crime squad, the Metropolitan Police's Computer Crime Unit. Its offices were set up in 1984 and were inevitably eventually visited by computer hackers.

19 Wolves Lane, Bounds Green, London, UK Street housing the former home of Gary McKinnon, where he carried out what the US claimed to be 'the biggest military hack of all time'.

20 Southwark Crown Court, 1, English Grounds, Southwark. London, UK Site of the (not always successful) prosecution of the UK's first hackers.

Ten hacking conferences

21 DEF CON Held in Las Vegas, this is the biggest hacker convention in the United States; held during the summer (June–August).

22 Chaos Communication Congress The oldest and Europe's largest hacker conference, held by Chaos Computer Club.

23 INFILTRATE Hosted by Immunity, Inc., this is a deep technical security conference that focuses on offensive technical issues. The conference has been held annually in Miami Beach, Florida, since 2011.

24 **Observe Hack Make** Dutch hacking conference that has been widely seen as the European philosophical conference for the alternative hacking community.

25 **The Hackers Conference** Held in New Delhi, this is India's biggest annual security conference.

26 **Ekoparty** A hacker convention in Argentina and one of the most important in South America; held annually around September in Buenos Aires.

27 **Hacktivity** Held in Budapest, Hungary, and run every September; the largest hacker conference in Central and Eastern Europe.

28 **Conferences held by** *2600* The oldest publication dedicated to hacking, set up in 1984, holds its Hackers on Planet Earth (HOPE) conferences in New York in July/August every other year.

29 **MALCON** The world's first International Malware Conference, hosted in India.

30 **Summercon** One of the oldest hacker conventions; held during summer (frequently in June). It helped set the ground for conferences such as HOPE and DEF CON.

Ten cyber crime fighting organizations

31 **European Cyber Crime Centre (EC3)** European centre dedicated to fighting cyber crime (www.europol.europa.eu/ec3)

32 **National Security Agency (NSA)** Lead US agency fighting cyber crime (www.nsa.gov/ia/index.shtml)

33 Federal Bureau of Investigation (FBI) Heavily involved in combating cyber crime (www.fbi.gov/about-us/investigate/cyber)

34 Virtual Global Taskforce fighting child exploitation online (www.virtualglobaltaskforce.com/)

35 McAfee Cybersafety Resource Portal private security firm (www.mcafee.com/us/campaigns/fight_cybercrime/cru/index.html)

36 Serious Organised Crime Agency, Britain UK's lead body overseeing fight against cyber crime (www.soca.gov.uk/threats/cyber-crime)

37 Kaspersky Russian multinational Internet security firm (www.kaspersky.com/)

38 Office central de lutte contre la criminalité liée aux technologies de l'information et de la communication (OCLCTIC) France's national cyber crime investigation unit

39 Mandiant security firm (www.mandiant.com/)

40 The International Association of Cyber Crime Prevention Founded in France, now an international body (www.cybercrime-en.org)

Ten films on cyber crime

41 *The Net* (1995) Starring Sandra Bullock as a systems analyst

42 *Antitrust* (2001) Pro open source thriller directed by Peter Howitt

43 *Disclosure* (1994) Starring Michael Douglas and Demi Moore – sex and the computer industry, in a story written by Michael Crichton. Who could ask for more?

44 *One Point 0* (2004) Acclaimed 'cyberpunk' science-fiction film directed by Jeff Renfroe and Marteinn Thorsson

45 *Die Hard 4: Live Free or Die Hard* (2007) Cyber baddies plan to hack the FBI, but first they have to beat Bruce Willis...

46 *Sneakers* (1992) All-star cast involving hackers and phone phreakers

47 *Wargames* (1983) About a young hacker who accidentally stumbles into the US military's main computer

48 *Tron* (1982) Cult science fiction film starring Jeff Bridges

49 *Swordfish* (2001) Hacker wanted by bank robbing gang because of his skills

50 *Enemy of the State* (2001) Full of conspiracy theories but still fun to watch

Ten non-fiction books on cyber crime

51 *Hackers, Heroes of the Computer Revolution* by Steven Levy (1984) A classic title on the history of the early hackers

52 *The Hacker's Handbook* 1980s classic text on real hacking incidents, with explanations. Peter Sommer, who wrote it under the pseudonym Hugo Cornwall, is now a respected academic.

53 *Cyber War: The Next Threat to National Security and What to Do about It* by Richard A. Clarke (2010) Security expert

Clarke explains how vulnerable the United States is to cyber criminals and spies.

54 *The Cuckoo's Egg: Tracking a Spy through the Maze of Computer Espionage* by Clifford Stoll (1989) First-person account of the hunt for a computer hacker

55 *Cybercrime: Criminal Threats from Cyberspace* by Susan W. Brenner (2010) Overview from a respected academic

56 *Ghost in the Wires: My Adventures as the World's Most Wanted Hacker* by Kevin Mitnick (2011) From perhaps the world's most famous hacker

57 *The Hacker Crackdown: Law and Disorder on the Electronic Frontier* by Bruce Sterling (1993) Charts the crackdown on hacking in the 1990s

58 *Masters of Deception: The Gang that Ruled Cyberspace* by Michele Slatalla (1995) Lively true story of electronic gang warfare and computer crimes between two rival groups of hackers

59 *Gray Hat Hacking: The Ethical Hacker's Handbook* by Shon Harris, Allen Harper, Chris Eagle and Jonathan Ness (2007) The latest strategies for uncovering hack attacks

60 *Kingpin: How One Hacker Took over the Billion-dollar Cybercrime Underground by* Kevin Poulsen (2011) Written by a hacker turned investigative reporter

Ten key milestones in the history of cyber crime

61 1978 – First electronic bulletin board system (BBS) appears and is soon the main means of communication for the electronic underground.

62 1981 – Ian Murphy, aka 'Captain Zap', becomes first US hacker to be tried as a felon, after breaking into AT&T's computers.

63 1981 – Elk Cloner, an Apple II boot virus, is written by a teenager and released into the 'wild'.

64 1988 – First National Bank of Chicago is the victim of an attempt to steal $70 million using computers.

65 1988 – Robert T. Morris launches a self-replicating worm (the Internet or Morris worm) on the fledgling Internet and it affects 6,000 networked computers.

66 1995 – Believed to be the year of the first recorded use of the term 'phishing' for emails that try to fool recipients into disclosing personal information.

67 1998 – First primitive distributed denial-of-service (DDoS) attacks on websites recorded.

68 2003 – Start of co-ordinated cyber attacks on American-based computers that lasted for at least three years and were given the name 'Titan Rain'.

69 2008 – Conventional military strike by Russians against Georgia coincides with cyber attack on same country from 'unknown' source...

70 2010 – Discovery of Stuxnet weaponized software at an Iranian uranium enrichment plant heralds new era in software warfare.

Ten destructive computer viruses and worms

71 **Internet (or Morris) worm** Took down the early internet in 1988 by accident...

72 **Storm worm** Sophisticated malware from 2007 that originally used the words '230 dead as storm batters Europe' in the subject line of email that sent it

73 **Melissa** Widespread macro virus that hit our screens and the headlines in 1999

74 **Sasser** In 2004 this worm caused widespread damage including blocking all 75 satellite communications for the news agency Agence France-Presse (AFP) and causing Delta Air Lines to cancel several transatlantic flights because its computer systems were overloaded.

75 **MyDoom** In 2004 this became the fastest-spreading email worm yet recorded.

76 **Conficker** First seen in 2008 and a problem all over the world. According to the Chinese authorities, 'Eighteen million Chinese computers have been infected by the Conficker virus every month.'

77 **Chernobyl** This virus (also known as CIH) triggers on April 26 each year, the anniversary of the Chernobyl nuclear disaster. Written by a student in Taiwan and released in 1998, it infected an estimated 60 million computers worldwide.

78 **ILOVEYOU (or Love Letter)** Released in the Philippines in 2000, this worm is said to have caused billions of dollars of damage around the world.

79 **Blaster worm** This 2003 worm hit Microsoft's Windows 2000 and Windows XP operating systems and is notable for containing a message aimed at the company's founder: 'Billy Gates why do you make this possible? Stop making money and fix your software!!'

80 **Red October** Discovered in October 2012, this discreet and highly sophisticated spyware may have been quietly stealing documents since 2007.

Ten famous hackers/cyber criminals

81 **John Draper** One of the famous 'phone phreakers' who hacked telephone networks

82 **Kevin Mitnick** The hacker who appeared on the FBI's 'most wanted' list

83 **Kevin Poulsen** A famed hacker turned investigative journalist

84 **Jonathan James** Hacker who obtained source code for the International Space Station while still a teenager

85 **Mafiaboy** (real name Michal Calce) Hacker who in 2000 launched denial-of-service attacks against Yahoo!, Dell, CNN and Amazon, among others. He was 16 at the time.

86 **Gary McKinnon** British hacker who in 2001 and 2002 launched what the US authorities said was the 'biggest military computer hack' of all time, targeting US military computers and NASA. He claims he was just looking for information on UFOs.

87 **Adrian Lamo** Gained notoriety in early 2000s by hacking into the *The New York Times*, Microsoft and Yahoo!

88 **Cameron Lacroix** Famously hacked Paris Hilton's mobile phone

89 **David L. Smith** The man who launched the Melissa virus on the world in 1999, though he did not write it.

90 **Albert Gonzalez** The man behind a huge US credit card fraud from 2005 to 2007, the biggest in the US at the time

Five spectacular hacks

91 In January 2010 it was revealed that Gmail accounts belonging to Chinese human rights activists and senior US government officials were hacked. Google's response was to threaten to shut down its Chinese operation and to state it would no longer censor its Chinese search engine.

92 On 21 October 2002 unknown hackers attempted to bring down Internet backbone with co-ordinated hour-long attack starting at 5 p.m. Four of the 13 Internet backbone servers matching domain names survived the attack and kept the Internet running.

93 In October 1989 WANK worm (Worms Against Nuclear Killers) hit NASA offices in Greenbelt, MD, in the United States and ran a banner across system computers in a protest against the launch of the plutonium-fuelled, Jupiter-bound *Galileo* probe.

94 During a period of three days in July 2009, the websites of South Korea's president, a large online auction house, a bank, the country's biggest daily newspaper, the White House, the Pentagon and many other targets came under DDoS attack from at least 166,000 computers in a botnet.

95 The Sony PlayStation Network was twice hacked in 2011, with more than 77 million user accounts compromised.

Five hackers in fiction

96 Lisbeth Salander, heroine of *The Girl with the Dragon Tattoo*, *The Girl Who Played with Fire* and *The Girl who Kicked the Hornets' Nest* by Stieg Larsson

97 Dennis Nedry, anti-hero hacker of Michael Crichton's classic *Jurassic Park*

98 Henry Dorsett Case, another anti-hero, this one from William Gibson's *Neuromancer*

99 Randy Waterhouse in American author Neal Stephenson's acclaimed 'geek' novel *Cryptonomicon*

100 Nick Haflinger in John Brunner's science-fiction novel *The Shockwave Rider*

Index

Acknowledgements

The authors and publisher would like to give their thanks for permission to reproduce the following images:

Chapter 3 Tim Berners-Lee © drserg/Shutterstock.com **Chapter 4** Office © Monkey Business Images/Shutterstock.com **Chapter 5** Email screen shot © Pixel 4 Images/Shutterstock.com **Chapter 6** Botnet visualization © Gunnar Assmy/Shutterstock.com **Chapter 8** Facebook © Pan Xunbin/Shutterstock.com **Chapter 9** Child at computer © Pressmaster/Shutterstock.com **Chapter 10** Natanz surveillance image © Digital Globe/Corbis Images.

The authors would also like to express their thanks to Howard Schmidt, former Cyber-Security Co-ordinator for US President Barack Obama, for permission to use (in Chapter 11) a quote taken from an interview with Peter Warren.

Milton Keynes UK
Ingram Content Group UK Ltd.
UKHW032341131024
449558UK00009B/87